The New Restaurant

The New Restaurant

DINING DESIGN 2

Charles Morris Mount

Architecture & Interior
Design Library

AN IMPRINT OF
PBC INTERNATIONAL, INC.

Distributor to the book trade in the United States and Canada
Rizzoli International Publications Inc.
300 Park Avenue South
New York, NY 10010

Distributor to the art trade in the United States and Canada
PBC International, Inc.
One School Street
Glen Cove, NY 11542

Distributor throughout the rest of the world
Hearst Books International
1350 Avenue of the Americas
New York, NY 10019

Library of Congress Cataloging–in–Publication Data

Mount, Charles Morris.
        The new restaurant: dining design 2 / by Charles Morris Mount.
            p.   cm.
        Includes index.
        ISBN 0–86636–241–X
        1. Restaurants--Decoration--United States.   I. Title.   II. Title:
NK2195.R4M68   1995
725' .71--dc20   94-24183
                                                                    CIP

CAVEAT– Information in this text is believed accurate, and will pose no problem for the student or
casual reader. However, the author was often constrained by information contained in signed release
forms, information that could have been in error or not included at all. Any misinformation (or lack
of information) is the result of failure in these attestations. The author has done whatever is possible
to insure accuracy.

Color separation by
Fine Arts Repro House Co., Ltd., H.K.

Printing and binding by
Toppan Printing Co., Ltd., H.K.

Printed in China

10 9 8 7 6 5 4 3 2 1

This book is dedicated to my many friends and colleagues
who got me "hooked" on restaurant design:
James Beard, who I considered the "King" of American food;
Julia Child, who Jim introduced me to, and her book Mastering the Art of
French Cooking; George Nelson, who gave me the opportunity to design
my first restaurant, La Potagerie; and to Jacques Pepin who guided me
through the amazing world of a restaurant.

CONTENTS

FOREWORD

Danny Meyer, *Proprietor*
Union Square Cafe and
Gramercy Tavern, New York

Restaurant design has become as compelling an element as menu, food, wine and staffing in determining a restaurant's success, and for good reason. No other component is as powerful in distinguishing the owner's intended atmosphere of hospitality and welcome.

Thanks to widespread travel, training and trade press, the level of cooking in America has risen to an extraordinary new level. So has the quality of restaurant wine lists, as winemakers have gained technical skills that put them on almost-equal footing with Mother Nature. The unintended downside of all this improvement in our restaurants' gastronomic product is a sad sameness and mediocre "me-too-ness" in the way the food tastes.

Since restaurant patrons are looking to be fed as much for emotional reasons as they are for gustatory ones, restaurant design is the final frontier for winning them over, and successful design must convey a very specific sense of welcome. Are guests welcome to relax or let loose? Are they welcome to conduct business or romance? Will the social setting welcome discretion or shall it encourage a theatrical set on which the guests are actors?

And how will the setting affect the staff's ability to provide warm hospitality? If a restaurant design is a forceful influence on how a guest feels during the course of one meal, imagine its impact on the employees who are required to conduct their otherwise stressful occupation there day after day, night after night. To be effective, restaurant design must strike a nearly impossible balance between three competing agendas: that of the guest, who must feel welcome, aroused and transported; that of the staff, which must be able to complete its tasks in a smooth, stress-free flow that allows for maximum hospitality; and that of the restaurant's owner, for in providing all this comfort for guests and staff, there must still remain the proper ratio of selling area to manufacturing space to allow for maximum profit.

Finally, no matter how good a design is, if its architect has imposed a personal vision and style, cookie-cutter fashion, rather than actively listening and responding to the personal needs of the end user, the long term success of the restaurant is in grave danger. Just like a home, a restaurant works best when the people dwelling in it have a natural emotional affinity to the hundreds of decisions that went into creating it. So long as winning restaurant design remains hospitality-driven, hand-crafted and specially tailored to each project, it will overcome the copycat dullness which now threatens the prominence of food as the primary reason people dine out.

Danny Meyer

INTRODUCTION

Food and Design are my passion in life. When I visit a new restaurant, cafe or diner, I turn over the plates to see who the manufacturer is, and I even go so far as to check out who manufactured the dining chair I'm sitting in by turning it upside down. Gathering such vital statistics is an ongoing part of my life and work.

This book blends the knowledge and experience I've gained as a professional designer and life-long dining enthusiast. Growing up in rural Alabama, I was steeped in the pleasures of Southern culinary traditions. Food played a major role in the Mount household, and it was my mother's magical kitchen that set the tone in those early years. Later, when I graduated from design school, I set out for Europe where I encountered the true art of dining—a blend of sumptuous food, glorious architecture and compelling ambience. These experiences shaped my interest in restaurant design and they continue to influence my work.

Today's trend toward informal dining is of special interest to me, in part because it recalls many happy hours spent in the casual bistros, wine bars and sidewalk cafes of Europe. The projects I have selected for this book show the astonishing variety of casual dining environments that can be enjoyed today throughout the world, from sophisticated urban bistros to classic American diners.

Each project is evaluated in terms of its basic concept, how it was developed and how well it works. I also look at ambience—the atmosphere and the mood

McDonald's, A&S Plaza, New York, New York
Photography by N. McGrath

Mr. Steak, Winston Salem, North Carolina
Photography by Scott Frances

created—and how it was achieved. A successful project is one that effectively combines design, food, lighting, colors, materials, finishes, and graphics to achieve a total, satisfying dining experience.

Floor plans, dimensions and budget information are cited throughout, clearly demonstrating that good design can be cost-effective. Many restaurants are now allocating space for retail purposes, adding another dimension to the diner's experience. Bars, open kitchens, and attractive food display areas are among the varied features frequently found in informal dining interiors.

As a restaurant designer, I aim for the successful marriage of food and design. The "best" projects are those in which food and design reinforce each other: they should not stand alone. This can only be achieved through careful planning. Clients are too often in a rush. They want to hurry through the design process and build the restaurant.

My advice is to slow down, work on the total concept and take the time necessary to make sure it works. If you spend time at the beginning of your project and lay these foundations well, you will be rewarded handsomely.

Since I entered the field in 1970, I have designed every type of food-related project you can imagine, from the futuristic McDonald's in a Manhattan department store to the retro Silver Diner in Maryland. Yet I can honestly say that I am still inspired by each new potential project. As you glance through the pages ahead, I hope that you will discover new ideas, that you will appreciate the

American Cafe, National Place, Washington, D.C.
Photography by H. Durston Saylor

quality shown in these outstanding projects, and that you will be inspired, as I am, by the power of good design.

Bon Appétit!

Charles Morris Mount

Canastels, New York, New York
Photography by Peter Paige

C H A P T E R   1

New Age

Local No-Chol

Westlake Village, California

Local No-Chol serves low-calorie, no-cholesterol, healthy food, and is interested in educating its customers about issues pertaining to health. They provide the nutritional breakdowns of their foods, and an open kitchen allows customers to view the preparation of fresh ingredients. There is a retail area featuring organic foods, as well as fun, playful retail items such as a galvanized-tin heart. The overall design statement is spare, yet warm due to the materials used. To accommodate a tight budget, the designers used the most economical plywood available for the sleek geometric walls. These are combined with a flashy galvanized metal ceiling with suspended bright spangles and plywood end-grain awnings. The entire design is geared to energize, and leave the guest with a feeling of harmony.

Size: 1,600 sq. ft.
Budget: $125/sq. ft.

Interior Designer
Muzingo Associates

Architect
Gina Muzingo, Muzingo Associates

Graphic Designer
Lisa King

Lighting/Kitchen Designer
Muzingo Associates

Contractor
BTS Construction

Restaurant Consultant
Richard Drapkin, The Restaurant Works

Photographer
Alex Vertikoff

below: The selling/serving area projects a rich warmth that is enhanced by low-voltage luminaires. An inlay of galvanized steel on the tabletops plays off the angular walls.

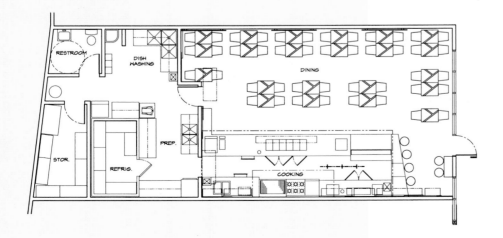

opposite: Shelving provides a sim yet effective way of displaying it for sale within the dining sp

right: Custom-fabricated from fiberglass and galvanized metal, sun-patterned wall sconces by Dan Sadler complement the textured hand-painted walls by Leslie Warren.

left: Indirect lighting extenuates the wall forms in this cozy corner.

above: Galvanized metal inset strips create a lively pattern on the various tabletops. The earthy-yellow, burnt-orange and cool-ocean-blue palette instills a sense of well being.

Felissimo Tearoom

New York, New York

The Tearoom at Felissimo is one of those unexpected pleasures found only in New York—both unexpected and absolutely charming. Every detail and all merchandising at Felissimo is unique and has a particular focus and awareness. This tearoom, with its natural, almost primitive feel, provides a quiet retreat from an intense city environment. It is very design conscious and keenly environmental. Tea is the main focus, and the food served—small sandwiches, scones, and cookies—works well with the varieties offered. The tea bar is fabricated of steel, and finished with a patina and wax seal. Copper is used in various counter areas, and there are large panels of sandblasted glass. All seating is custom-fabricated from cherry wood, and the tables have custom-crafted bronze bases and cherry tops. The colored concrete floor complements the walls which are treated with specialist paint and murals. A flexible lighting system which is used throughout the store highlights a display from the Republic of Tea. White noise is provided by a small custom-designed fountain.

Size: 750 sq. ft.

Interior Designer
Clodagh

Architect
Robert Pierpont

Graphic Designer
Studio N

Lighting Designer
Johnson Schwinghammer

Contractor
Kajima International

Photographer
Daniel Aubry

above: The wall painting has a primitive aspect, and is very calming. Dry teas for sale are displayed at the tea bar which also serves as a hospitality station for waiters.

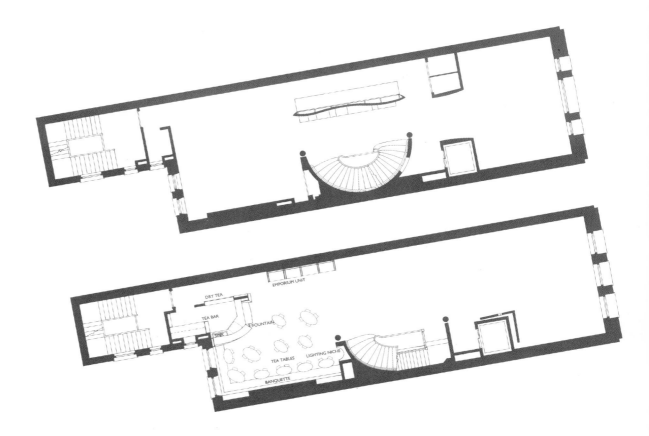

opposite: Names of teas are stenciled into the patina of the steel tea bar.

Rockenwagner

Santa Monica, California

Interior Designer/Architect
David Kellen, Architect

Lighting Designer
David Kellen, Architect

Kitchen Designer
Wolfgang Design

Contractor
Fadi and Sami Shabshab

Photographer
Tim Street-Porter

Rockenwagner is located in a development designed by Frank Gehry, of which the Santa Monica Museum of Art is the cornerstone. His design integrates new structures with ones constructed as warehouses in the 1920s. Located in one of these beautiful old warehouses, Rockenwagner already had elaborate roof trusses, wood-beamed ceilings, and monumental space to work with—a designer's dream come true.

The design concept for this restaurant is a town square, in a very abstract fashion. All the architectural elements are carefully placed so they read as a sculptural installation within the confines of the 1920s volume. The exterior walls of the kitchen and serving areas—covered with materials such as exterior stucco, logs, bricks, and slate—read as building forms to further convey the abstraction of a courtyard.

The restaurant is owned by Hans Rockenwagner who was instrumental in promoting California cuisine. The open kitchen, which adds to the overall atmosphere and spirit of the restaurant, is Chef Rockenwagner's new stage.

A collaboration between local artists and the architect, the freestanding lighting poles create a playful, fun extension of the town square idea, as they become street signs and lamp posts. Additional illumination is provided by track lighting mounted on trusses in the ceiling.

Size: 3,500 sq. ft.
Budget: $65/sq. ft.

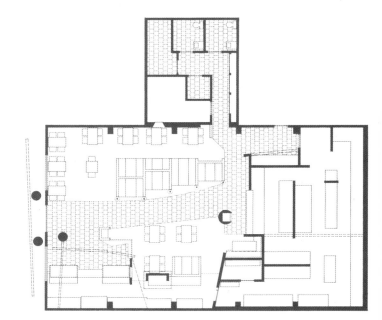

right: **Many interesting architectural compositions are found within the confines of Rockenwagner. Note the angled wine rack on the far wall.**

right: The long open window looking into the kitchen showcases the culinary talents of Chef Rockenwagner. The architecture has a Southwest American flavor.

left: Various architectural elements and the use of common building materials reflect the town square theme of Rockenwagner. This overall view looks toward the front of the restaurant.

Fama
Santa Monica, California

Interior Designer/Architect
David Kellen, Architect

Graphic Designer
Gene Fama

Lighting Designer
David Kellen, Architect

Kitchen Designer
Hans Rockenwagner

Contractor
Asterisk Construction

Photographer
Tim Street-Porter

Fama is an 1,800-square-foot restaurant in Santa Monica, California. From the exterior, the restaurant presents a warm playful ambience, and the expansive open storefront displays the sculptural quality of the interior. Based on an urban courtyard concept, the interior layout defines a series of inter-acting spaces. Upon entering the restaurant, a path of gridded floor covering leads to the maitre d's desk and a small bar beyond. Overhead, a floating canopy suggests that "you have arrived." The wood-clad columns show how the designers used a very simplistic indus-trial material—plywood—to create a rich, warm and playful sculptural design. The rear wall of the restaurant completes the abstract composition in a styl-ish, yet minimal way.

Fama's lighting design utilizes a very flexible, low-voltage cable system by Ingo Maurer. The color of the exposed bulbs adds to the overall warmth of Fama.

Size: 1,800 sq. ft.
Budget: $60/sq. ft.

opposite: **The volume of the space is dramatically enlarged and made more interesting with the plywood-clad columns. Note the canopy at the maitre d's stand near the entry.**

right: **This is a detail of the column and beam sculpture at the ceiling line. Note the entry pavilion.**

left: **From the exterior one is aware of the sculptural quali-ty of Fama's interior environ-ment. The facade fits quite neatly into a 1930's art deco building.**

The Salad Bowl

New York, New York

The Salad Bowl is a take-out and self-service cafe located in the heart of Times Square, New York City. The menu features freshly prepared salads, various baked goods, frozen yogurt, and other light fare. Four Kurdish brothers who own a number of other such cafes throughout New York City own and operate The Salad Bowl. Times Square is filled with all the national fast-food chains, so in order for The Salad Bowl to compete, the design had to express a combination of fun and excitement, along with an appealing display for food items.

The display counters and open kitchen located in the front allow the maximum amount of product exposure in the narrow storefront area. A perforated, back-lit serpentine shroud above the open kitchen signals the main area for serving and presenting food. Dining room seating and service areas occupy the remaining space. Two large decorative "bowl" forms, painted in beautiful "Matisse-like" patterns and colors, dominate and break-up the long dining room. The riot of color and pattern makes them festive and fun. Alvar Aalto's birch chairs, and birch-plywood tabletops are used in the dining area. The ceiling is gypsum board painted a soft green.

At the rear of the cafe, a large pear made of natural birch wood adds another wonderfully rich piece of unexpected whimsy. The pear is cut in half to reveal the seed and core on the back side. A combination of wall washers and downlights is used for the lighting. Very warm and inviting, The Salad Bowl is unlike any other salad bar/cafe you will find in New York City.

Size: 3,900 sq. ft.

Interior Designer/Architect
Hugh A. Boyd, A.I.A., Boyd Associates

Graphic Designer
Susan Roberts, Art Color Design

Lighting Designer
Alfred R. Borden, IV, IALD

Kitchen Designer
Boyd Associates

Contractor
Steglia Group, Inc.

Photographer
Dub Rogers

above: **The logo's black on white design relates to the overall design of the space, reinforcing the total concept.**

opposite: **Made of natural birch wood, a great pear provides a wonderfully rich unexpected piece of whimsy.**

right: **The open cooking area, front counters with food displays, stainless steel shroud and gypsum-board floating ceiling are immediately noticeable upon entering The Salad Bowl.**

This view toward the front of
the cafe and its Broadway
facade shows the bowl and
pear with its core and seed.

opposite: **Graphic forms reminiscent of Matisse come across in the "salad bowls."**

above: **The "bowl" forms are voluptuous and enticing, and the pear is appealing and fun. The Aalto chairs and the tables together create one rich design idea with great graphics.**

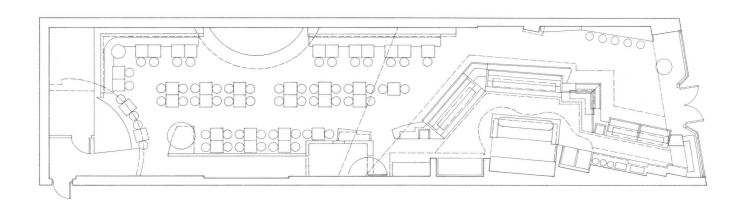

Stars

Frankfurt, Germany

Interior Designers/Architects
Jordan Mozer, Mike Suomi,
Diane MacCewen, Larry Traxler,
Jeff Carloss of Jordan Mozer &
Associates, Ltd.
Grisela Pauche-Garber (*consulting local architect*)

Graphic Designer
Martin Glomm

Lighting/Kitchen Designers
Jordan Mozer, Mike Suomi,
Diane MacCewen, Larry Traxler,
Jeff Carloss of Jordan Mozer and
Associates, Ltd.

Construction Management
Jordan Mozer & Associates, Ltd.
Ernst Kraft

Photographer
Helmut Mitter

Stars was inspired by another Mozer project, Cypress Club, in San Francisco. A name such as "Stars" would make one assume the obvious—that Hollywood stars are the focus of the concept. Mozer took a different approach, however. His inspiration was *A Brief History of Time* by Stephen Hawking, and the big bang theory. Owner Ernst Kraft's request that Mozer create an "American" restaurant led to the exploration of American Pop Culture of the late '50s and early '60s. Detroit was a major contributor to the design idea with its "rocket engine" cars like Ford Galaxy, Starliner and Starfire. Mozer studied profiles, fittings, dashboards and all for inspiration. Comic books and science fiction movies from this period were also design contributors.

Lighting fixtures take on the shapes of imaginary asteroids and comets, and the design motifs are also found on the floor patterns. The relief sculpture at the periphery has abstractions of spaceships,

comets, planets and rayguns from the comics. The restaurant is very sleek and angular and the overall coloring of the space recalls the two-tone paint jobs on 1950s American cars.

Stars is located in the basement of the MesseTurm, the tallest building in Europe, and the site of trade exhibitions and shows that attract over four million visitors each year. The customer base is not only international visitors, but also corporate tenants of the office tower and other locals. Herr Kraft, is responsible for introducing "California Cuisine" to Frankfurt.

Size: 8,900 sq. ft.
Budget: $185/sq. ft

above **Lighting enhances the appearance of both patron and food with custom-designed fixtures.**

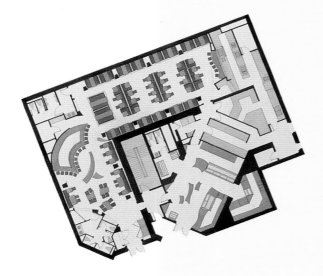

left: The ceiling design best illustrates the big bang theory with gyrating lights breaking away from ceiling beams, which are breaking away from the girders.

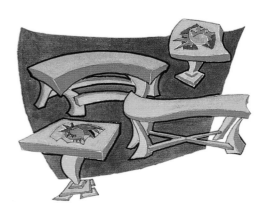

above: Lighting forms in the ceiling take the shape of comets, which are repeated in the floor patterns.

right: Lighting creates a mesmerizing effect at Stars, minimizing the shortcomings of a low-ceiling basement space with no natural light.

Kachina Grill

Los Angeles, California

Located in the atrium of a downtown Los Angeles office building, Kachina Grill is a restaurant where the food concept and design statement are American Southwest. Architectural elements are abstractions of plateau landscapes and buildings, and convey the feeling of a stage set. The original ceiling was low and filled with mechanical equipment, ducts and electrical pipes. To expand the mind's concept of the low confining space, the designer chose to use only the grid of the ceiling and remove the tiles. The grid and ductwork above were then painted in contrasting colors, reminiscent of the ceiling of a small theater.

Plaster on architecturally sculptured walls recalls colors and textures found in the desert Southwest, and a slate floor adds to the natural tones of the restaurant. Simple, spare furnishings and halogen spotlights further the stage set look. Cooking is done over open-fire grills.

Size: 6,000 sq. ft.
Budget: $85/sq. ft.

Interior/Lighting Designer
David Kellen, Architect

Kitchen Designer
Avery Restaurant Supply

Contractor
JAL

Photographer
Ross Rappaport

above: **The entrance greets customers with strong architectural forms, colors, and art.**

right: **Kachina Grill's front desk and open kitchen are separated by walls that suggest the adobe structures of the desert Southwest.**

above: Shaped plaster walls
frame the bar, creating a com-
pound—a corral. The addi-
tion of red at the ceiling soffit
creates a color change in the
bar.

Tiles were left out of the ceiling's gridwork to create the effect of opening up a low, confining space.

CHAPTER  2

A Quick Bite

Pi's Place

Miami, Florida

Pi's Place is a restaurant/cafeteria located on the 11th floor of a high-rise tower in downtown Miami. Overlooking a lush garden and reflecting pool, the cafeteria offers a quick breakfast and lunch with the atmosphere and careful attention to detail of a fine restaurant. Pi's Place is entered through the self-service area, which contains separate serving tables clad in honed English slate. Small white hanging pendant lights highlight the food displays. Rather than the usual metal strips for tray slides, stainless steel buttons are set into a honed slate shelf. Rich sycamore wall panels, punched with small spaces, allow light into the servery.

Interior Designer/Architect
Gensler and Associates/Architects

Photographer
Nick Merrick, Hedrich-Blessing

above: **One of the dining areas in this 11th-floor sky lobby overlooks a lush tropical garden.**

left: **The dining rooms are carpeted in a dark green color that is repeated in the honed slate, polished marble dining tables, and mahogany slat-backed chairs' colorful tapestry.**

left: The unique treatment of the tray slides in the servery and entrance areas illustrates the functional design and close attention to detail found at Pi's Place.

below: Rich sycamore wall panels, punched with small spaces, allow light into the servery.

above: A curvilinear structure creates smaller, more intimate dining areas within the large volume.

Union Bank of Switzerland Cafeteria

New York, New York

Located on the 27th floor, the Union Bank of Switzerland Cafeteria has tremendous views of Manhattan and the surrounding environs. The building's central core dictated that all activities occur around the perimeter. Beginning at the elevator, the circulation plan continues in one direction around the floor, with the servery and general seating areas to the north and west, and executive dining rooms facing eastward. A diamond-shaped freestanding serving unit in the center of the servery displays the salad, dessert, and espresso bar, as well as a frozen yogurt machine, and soda fountain. A cold entrées display case, hot food area, and gourmet sandwich board are also located within the servery. At the very end of this one-way circulation there is a dish drop-off. Serving all the dining rooms on the entire floor, the central kitchen required a large part of the budget since installing ventilation and exhaust systems in the middle of a building is far more difficult than at either the ground or top floors.

Size: 19,000 sq. ft.

Interior Designers/Architects
Walter A. Hunt, Dina Frank
Jacob Bousso, Ana Gonzalez
Imelda Cancio, Uday Deshmukh of
Gensler and Associates/Architects

Lighting Designer
Cline, Bettridge, Bernstein

Photographer
Wolfgang Hoyt

right & above: **Stile and rail doors with opaque glass panels provide an elegant entrance into the executive dining rooms. Fabric-wrapped interior walls are hung with the bank's collection of contemporary Swiss artwork.**

right: Frosted glass panels placed atop banquettes parallel to the avenue create a sense of privacy and allow outside light to penetrate the innermost dining room.

left: Circulation through the servery is organized around a central diamond-shaped island displaying the main entrees.

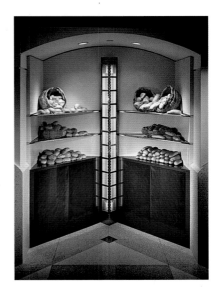

right: Easily-accessed alcoves located around the servery contain baked goods and other items.

left: Existing structural columns were augmented, creating a colonnade that efficiently directs traffic between seating areas.

above: Employees of the bank use computer-coded cards to gain access to the cafeteria.

right: Black marble diamonds and squares of grey terrazzo create a geometric floor pattern that is articulated by inlaid stainless steel strips.

Matador Bookstore Expansion

Northridge, California

Matador Bookstore Expansion is located in a shopping complex at California State University. This "scramble-style" cafeteria offers a variety of foods, including salads, pizza, grilled chicken and ice cream. Dramatic lighting, sculptural elements, and bright colors contribute to the exciting, fast-paced atmosphere. Most of the dining seating is located out-of-doors, situated to allow a smooth flow of pedestrian traffic.

Interior Designer
Samuel Carson

Architect
Coleman/Caskey Architects, Inc.

Graphic Designer
On the Edge

Lighting Designer
Toft, Wolff, Farrow, Inc.

Kitchen Designer
Hatch Design Group

Contractor
Whiting Turner Contracting, Co.

Photographer
Larry Falke

above: A cubby unit for packages and bags is one of the colorful sculptural elements strategically placed in the concourse.

right: The use of color and graphics is evident in this view of the concourse seating area.

above: **Continuous fluorescent architectural strips hung askew and metal halide lighting over food presentation areas contribute to the high-tech atmosphere of the servery.**

Bank of America Cafeteria

Phoenix, Arizona

Bank of America Cafeteria is located in a large credit card manufacturing and processing campus. The murals of fruits and vegetables are playful, and the colors used throughout are crisp, clean and sparkling— sunflower-yellow walls, the blue servery counter front and the off-white ceramic tile floor. Utilitarian stainless steel takes on a new and elegant style. Architectural elements were introduced to the cafeteria and servery areas by adding beams in the ceiling which also serve as a transition between the two ceiling heights.

Size: 18,000 sq. ft.

Interior Designer/Architect
Gensler and Associates/Architects

Photographer
Bob Swanson

right: The design team introduced architectural elements to the cafeteria and servery by adding beams in the ceiling; these serve as a transition between the two ceiling heights.

44

below: The mural of fruits
and vegetables creates the
personality of this corporate
servery.

York Galleria

York, Pennsylvania

York Galleria is a food court located in a 750,000-square-foot mall in York, Pennsylvania. National and local food vendors provide a broad range of specialty and fast foods. The palette, graphics and decor create an ambience that is fun and creative. Decorative column covers—with the graphic checkerboard idea first called out on the food court sign—are spot-lit with 100-watt bulbs.

Everything was fabricated in-house and installed at night during a four-day period to avoid any down time for the food court, and the decorative three-dimensional graphics had to be added to the existing structure without demolition.

Size: 62,162 sq. ft. (common area)
5,600 sq. ft. (seating area)

Interior Designer/Architect
T L Horton Design, Inc.

Graphic Designer/Contractor
T L Horton Design, Inc.

Photographer
Barth Tilloston, Barth Tilloston Photography

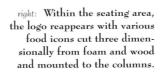

above: **Made of wood and silk screened to resemble a banner, this 7-foot horizontal sign identifies the food court and sets the design tone.**

right: **Within the seating area, the logo reappears with various food icons cut three dimensionally from foam and wood and mounted to the columns.**

right: **Common seating areas take up a large amount of space within the food court.**

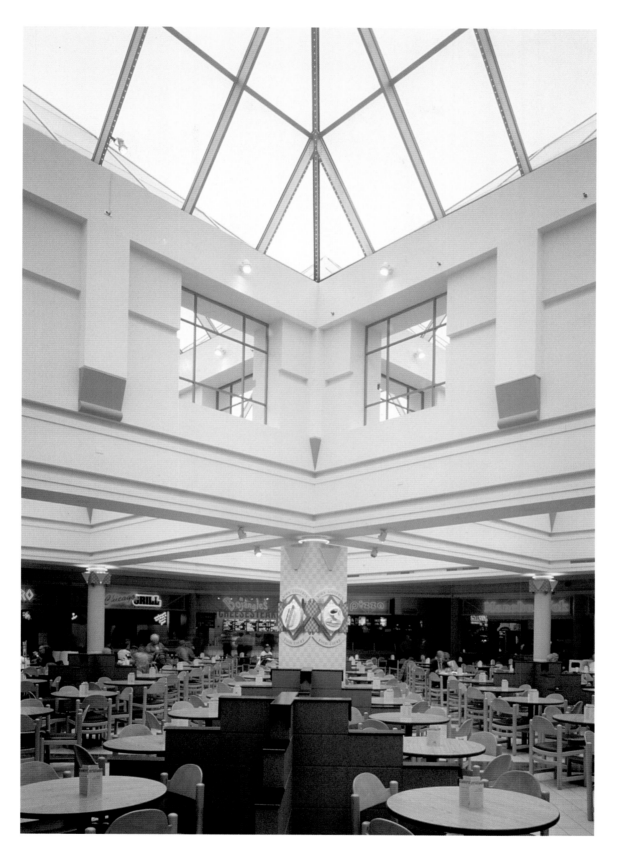

above: The large atrium-type skylight brings in copious amounts of natural daylight, and at night the mood of this space is dramatically changed by other lighting.

Union Station

Indianapolis, Indiana

Union Station is a food court located on the upper of two levels of retail shops connected to an office and hotel. A festive dining area for unique fast food prepared by local vendors, this food court is housed in the train shed of the old station in downtown Indianapolis. The original train tracks were left in place and are visible in the brick floors. A festive ambience is created by the bright colors of store fronts, banners, and signs.

The redesign had to be approved by the historical society, and no additions could be permanently attached to the original structure. The approximately 70,000 square feet of shops and food vendors is very linear by nature, with food stalls on one side and retail shops on the other. A 40-foot "train" dining car contains 20 booths of additional seating, and the ends can accommodate small bands for entertainment.

Size: 70,000 sq. ft.
(retail shops and food court)
Budget: $450,000 (food court)

Interior Designer/Architect
T L Horton Design, Inc.

Graphic Designer/Contractor
T L Horton Design, Inc.

Photographer
Joe Aker, Aker Photography

above: The palette of 12 colors used on the ceiling increased the food court's light levels, eliminating the need for new lighting. Skylights, arches, banners, and clocks all contribute to the fun and festive feeling at Union Station.

left: Freestanding, vertical directories are strategically placed throughout the vast main hall.

left: Elegant in form and texture, this is one of the major arches that supports the shed roof.

below: Neon-lit signage in the logo was pressure fit, and does not attach directly to the original metal work.

right: Stanchion signs inform visitors about the historical aspects of the train shed.

right & above: Made of wood with metal trim detail around the windows, poles and supports, this full-size train has a yellow prismax top canopy.

Cafe Briacco

Boston, Massachusetts

Cafe Briacco is adjacent to the lobby of an office building with which it shares similar materials. Stained maple casework and textured plaster walls complement the marble floor with many small-scale inlay patterns. The palette is warm and reflects the Mediterranean menu. Custom-designed lighting—directed toward solid horizontal and vertical surfaces—creates a theatrical contrast to the dark ceiling voids which expose the building's bones. Varying ceiling heights define the cafe's two separate seating areas, full service kitchen and servery.

Size: 2,100 sq. ft.
Budget: $220,000

Interior Designer/Archtect
Michael R. Davis AIA,
Bergmeyer Associates, Inc.

Lighting Designer
Bergmeyer Associates, Inc.

Contractor
Shawmut Design & Construction

Photographer
Lucy Chen

below: The diagonal mosaic augments the marble floor grid, and is suggested in the casework. Hanging low-voltage lights and custom-designed ceiling fixtures are among the many types of lighting used at this level.

above: Very dramatic and sculptural, this space is enhanced by unique lighting and the pattern inlay in the floor. The deep red color of the recessed panel is used throughout the cafe.

McDonald's at the Denton House

New Hyde Park, New York

McDonald's twelve thousandth store is located in the 125-year-old Denton House which formerly housed many other food facilities. The local community had a great deal of input in preserving and restoring this landmark building. Since there was nothing of merit to rescue from the interior, the designers tried to incorporate elements that suggested the past interior design. The most obvious challenge was to create a successful marriage between the existing structure and the restaurant chain's particular needs.

The center of the existing building was opened up to create a large, dramatic atrium space. The designers chose to develop a "house-within-a-house" concept, preserving the landmarked exterior and creating a more contemporary interior. This created an exciting set of contrasts. Cool-blue and warm-amber metal halide uplights are set into the cornice around the atrium's second level, and project toward the trusses and ceiling for a dramatic play of light and shadow during evening business hours.

Size: 6,300 sq. ft.
Budget: $2,000,000

Interior Designers
Jay Haverson, David Rockwell,
Carol DiCicco Vinci, James Ahn of
Haverson/Rockwell Architects P.C.

Architect
Raymond F. Fellman Architects

Lighting Designer
Haverson/Rockwell Architects P.C.

Contractor
Testa & Wirth Inc.

Photographer
Paul Warchol Photography

below: **Signage has been carefully integrated with the overall structure of the building.**

below: **This 19th-century house on Long Island was restored to become the twelve thousandth McDonald's store.**

opposite: **The veranda provides a comfortable dining area for customers.**

above: Adjacent to the mezzanine dining area, this children's party room has multicolored floor tiles, festive millwork, and a blue ceiling with stars.

below: **Exposed open trusses in the atrium add to the overall airy and spacious feeling.**

Dino's Cafe

La Jolla, California

Dino's Cafe is a retrofit restaurant on the lower lobby level of a corporate office building in the La Jolla Center. The design team wanted to create a cafe from adjoining spaces which had included a vending machine area, an outdoor patio, and a corridor connecting the parking garage to the main lobby. The food services, dining, and retail functions were to be unified and consolidated, while allowing passage without the sense of walking through the middle of a restaurant. There are 100 seats in this upscale fast-food dining room, and the atmosphere is very European. Gourmet pizzas, cappuccino, salads, and all types of pastries are served, while fine wines, baguettes and a variety of European magazines are retailed. The ambience extends into the lobby where tables and chairs set up for patrons create a sidewalk-cafe atmosphere within the confines of this corporate envelope. Security is achieved through the use of counters, low walls with 5-inch openings, and reverse displays.

Size: 4,000 sq. ft.

Interior Designer/Architect
BSHA Design Group, Inc.

Lighting Designer
Ray System

Graphic Designers
BSHA Design Group, Inc.
Nicholson Design

Contractor
Nielsen Construction &
Brodwolf Construction

Kitchen Designer
Amfab

Photographer
Bill Robinson

below: **A sidewalk cafe effect is achieved in this upscale fast-food dining room.**

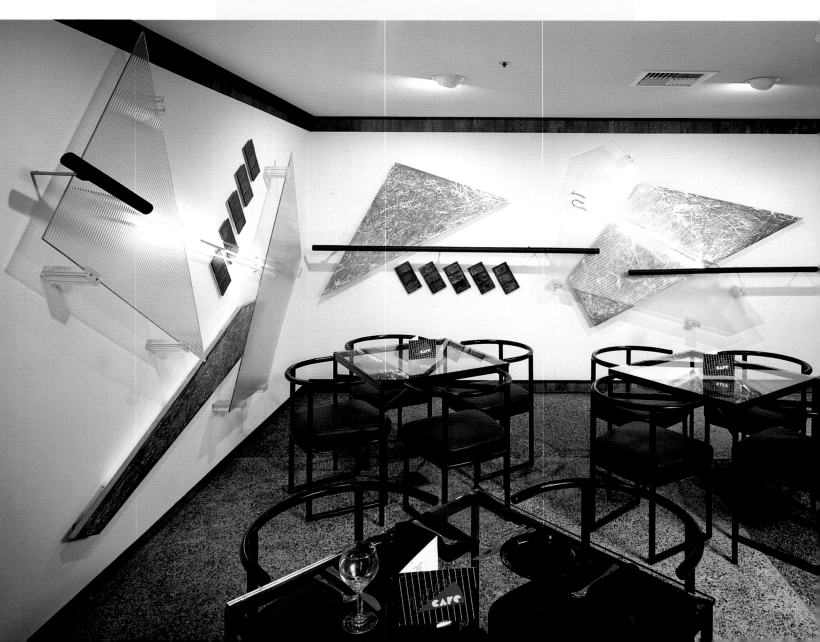

left: Dino's Cafe is located in the lower lobby level of this building in California's La Jolla Center.

right: Security is achieved through the use of counters, low walls with 5-inch openings, and reverse displays.

Baldini's Restaurant

Avon, Massachusetts

Baldini's is a fantasy of what an Italian diner would look like. A place with a high energy level, it is fun and lively, yet comfortable and intimate—all at the same time! Baldini's was originally conceived as primarily a take-out place in the suburbs, but market demand increased the "dine-in" segment and changed the business plan. The owners have two other Baldini's, and this is their first free-standing unit.

This unit is located at the gateway to a suburban shopping development, so the exterior had to convey a sense of excitement. It also had to say Italian food—pizza, sandwiches, salads and daily specials. The environment is Italian in an original way without being "Tuscan" or "Milanese." It is like the stage of an Italian opera set in a 1990s diner in the USA.

Budget: $550,000

Interior Designer/Architect
Design Continuum Inc.

Graphic Designers
Design Continuum Inc.
Adkins Balchunas

Lighting Designer
Design Continuum Inc.

Kitchen Designer
Al McDonald,
Tigar Restaurant Supply

Contractor
Cafco Construction

Photographer
Warren Jagger Photography

left: Arched structural details increase the height of the building, improving visibility from the road.

right: A multitude of plastic laminates, metal moldings, a colorful array of glazed tiles, and vinyl patterned floors further the Italian diner concept.

above: **Over the open display kitchen, a mural pokes fun at the owners, illustrating their restaurant history.**

CHAPTER  3

International

Vong

New York, New York

Jean Georges Vongerichten is the owner and chef of this French/Thai restaurant. The space was designed to support and complement the exotic, colorful and unusual food served. At the entry, a wall collage composed of fragments of stamps, currency, wallpaper, and artifacts ties the bar area in with the dining room and seems to tell a story. Randomly placed blown-glass lighting fixtures recall the Thai Festival of Lights and give the gold leaf ceiling and corresponding textured walls a mystical glow. Numerous Thai architectural elements are used as set pieces, such as a tatami platform that accommodates private parties or several couples at one long table, and an altar table with an intriguing array of raw spices and fruits displayed in footed dishes. One specialty booth is framed by a curved mosaic screen made of materials that recall an ancient Thai temple.

Size: 4,000 sq. ft.
Budget: $350,000

Interior Designer/Architect
Haverson/Rockwell Architects, P.C.

Graphic/Lighting Designer
Haverson/Rockwell Architects, P.C.

Contractor
Bronx Storefront Construction

Photographer
Paul Warchol Photography

below: Louvered dividers, painted in bright Thai colors, provide a sense of privacy in the raised tatami dining area.

left: A thoughtful and elegant display of the marriage of French and Thai flavorings is an appropriate element in Vong.

left: A collage of stamps, wallpaper, currency and artifacts at the entry connects a separate bar area with the dining room.

right: The main dining room has a warm ambience, due in part to lighting and wall color. Exotic green marble tabletops and reupholstered chairs add further dimension to Vong's design.

Kin Khao

New York, New York

Kin Khao, which translates into "Eat Rice," is based on owner Brad Kelley's research of market-style restaurants throughout Thailand. He wanted this Thai restaurant to be a "joint," as indigenous to Bangkok as to the SoHo section of Manhattan in which it is located. Diners become part of Kin Khao's decorative statement, rather than feeling incidental to gaudy finishes and seething dragons found in typical Oriental restaurants in the US.

The open kitchen—providing a culinary spectacle with smoke, spice and drama—is contained on two sides by an eating bar that encourages single dining. Across from the kitchen, an oak and mahogany bar with ornate carvings and beveled mirrors typical of turn-of-the-century New York taverns completes the axis around which all activity revolves.

Size: 1,800 sq. ft.
Budget: $75/sq. ft.

Interior Designer/Architect
L. Bogdanow & Associates, Architects

Graphic Designer
Susan Rose

Lighting/Kitchen Designer
L. Bogdanow & Associates, Architects

Contractor
D/E Construction Services

Photographer
Ross Muir

below: **Paraffin-fueled chrome "candle" sconces, inserted randomly in the painted brick walls of the long dining room, contribute to the understated lighting design. Food displays, table settings, and various wood textures add further interest.**

64

above: Found in a cellar on Staten Island, this oak and mahogany bar features ornate carvings and beveled mirrors typical of 19th-century New York taverns.

Anzu

Dallas, Texas

Serving Pacific Rim cuisine, Anzu embodies a diverse mix of cultures. The owner's grandfather was a noted chef who fled China during the Cultural Revolution, and later settled in Japan where he operated 35 restaurants. His father currently runs a traditional Japanese restaurant in America. With this background in the restaurant industry, Anzu's owner and manager has contributed to the unique cuisine which blends East and West, old and new—with the added twist of a chef trained in Italy.

Delivering excellent food and service at a reasonable cost in a casual but intriguing environment, Anzu attracts a wide range of customers—from formally dressed theater-goers to casually dressed diners.

Feng shui, an ancient Chinese geomancy that promotes well-being through the creation of harmonious environments, plays a key role in Anzu's design. For example, the designers had originally proposed to expose the ceiling structure as a way of adding visual height and saving money, but the *feng shui* expert brought in for consultation suggested that the designers close up and finish the ceiling, or add additional beams to "confuse and disguise" the actual building structure. The solution was to fill the ceiling void with thousands of handmade origami cranes contributed by friends, relatives and the designers to distract attention from the structure.

The exterior and interior walls are cement stucco with a warm-patinated finish. Lichen-green paper covering the first 18 inches of the interior walls adds a sense of scale and recalls the decorative use of paper applied to the bottom of mud walls found in traditional Japanese tea huts.

Size: 3,011 sq. ft.
Budget: $100/sq. ft.

right: **Cement stucco covers most of Anzu's facade with the exception of the entrance pylon which is clad in deep-blue square slate tiles. The gold-leaf letters are elegant against the stone background.**

Interior/Lighting Designer
Paul Draper and Associates, Inc.

Architect
John E. Wheeler Architects

Graphic Designer
David Carter Graphic Design Associates

Kitchen Designer
Judy Chin

Contractor
Luminous Corporation

Photographer
Klein & Wilson Photography

above: A vertical gold-leafed rectangle serves as a background for an antique wood carving of a running fox.

right: A series of booths is made almost private by the translucent white fabric that hangs between each.

left: Floating through the exposed trusses in the ceiling, the origami cranes symbolize long life in Japan. Ingo Maurer chandeliers complement the checkerboard wall and gridded floor pattern in this Pacific Rim design.

Simplicity at its best, the bar features a concrete base and red-lacquered wood top. The area behind the bar is open to a sushi preparation area where the chef can be seen at work.

Bitu

Bamberg, Germany

A casual bistro/cafe with no fixed menu, Bitu features à la carte, seasonal delicacies. There is a lively interaction between the existing building and Bitu's avant-garde design, with elements of a bygone era restored and integrated into the modern design concept.

Perforated sheet and stainless steel lighting sculptures on the walls and columns, unconventional room layouts, extravagant use of materials and finishes, and careful attention to detail all contribute to the modern, high-tech feel of Bitu.

Interior Designer/Architect
dirk obliers design

Graphic/Lighting Designer
dirk obliers design

Contractor
Friedhelm Hübner

Photographer
Dirk Obliers

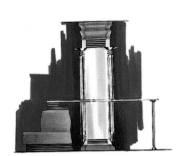

left and above: **The designer has successfully integrated the existing building structure with Bitu's contemporary design.**

right: The reflective ceiling treatment and round seating element enhance Bitu's contemporary atmosphere.

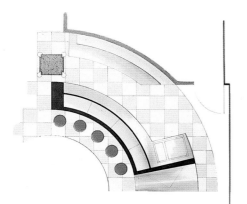

right: The palette creates a total composition in which new and old are simultaneously contrasted and integrated.

opposite: Expansive windows and a different design approach give this indoor dining space an out-of-doors feel.

left: Custom-made perforated sheet and stainless steel lighting sculptures are used on walls and columns. The stainless steel table beyond is a work of art.

above: Bitu's reflective walls and pillars visually expand the space, while mirroring makes the ceiling look twice its height.

right: Elements of bygone ages have been carefully restored and integrated into the modern design concept.

above: **Direct lighting from halogen dot sources creates drama, while indirect lighting provides a warm atmosphere.**

Tai Pan

Cambridge, Massachusetts

The combination of a restaurant serving northern China's spicy dishes and southern China's seafood specialties with a Japanese-originated karaoke lounge has created this hybrid food and entertainment establishment.

A continuous freestanding curved "wall" of columns divides the area into three zones, with dining areas on both sides, and a corridor running along it. Each space has its own unique character and ambience, yet the openness of the "wall" creates a harmonious dialogue. The corridor, inspired by the surrounding urban environment, becomes a "street" connecting the two dining areas. At one end of the corridor, an oversized mirror reflects the city outside, while at the other, the entrance with its 15-foot-high maple coffered ceiling greets guests. Creating the other side of the corridor, a series of abstracted facades, small-scaled fenestrations, and trellis roof overhangs makes the "street" more magical.

The dining area outside of the curved wall faces a city street and park. Enveloped by the curved wall, the other dining area is more intimate, and contains the bar and performance area for karaoke. Being a geometric study of positive and negative space, plane and volume, scale and proportion, lightness and darkness, and color and texture, the design contributes to the metaphor of yin and yang, an idea appropriate to Tai Pan.

Interior Designer/Architect
Lawrence Man Architect

Lighting Designer
Lawrence Man Architect

Kitchen Designer/Contractor
MCM

Photographer
Lucy Chen

below: **This facade fronts the shopping mall. The columns, alternating colors and forms, and almost subdued signage reflect Tai Pan's interior design.**

above: **The design of the bar area is simple and straightforward.**

opposite: **Shelving inserted in the curved wall provides patrons waiting to be seated with a convenient place to set their drinks.**

The curved wall of columns provides division without creating a closed or fragmented design.

left: Trellis roof overhangs enliven the wall that defines the kitchen and supporting functions, and the decorative screen doors open to a buffet table.

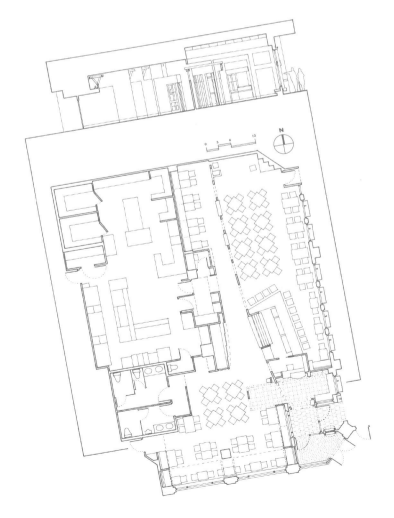

below: The entry area, intersected by the curved wall, features a 15-foot-high, up-lit vaulted ceiling. All the forms, planes, colors, and positive and negative spaces contribute to the yin-yang design concept.

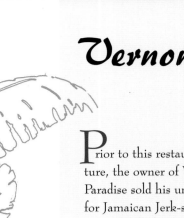

Vernon's Jerk Paradise

New York, New York

Prior to this restaurant venture, the owner of Vernon's Jerk Paradise sold his unique sauces for Jamaican Jerk-style cuisine at his small shop in the Bronx. For his first restaurant venture, he wanted to provide a tropical dining atmosphere in midtown Manhattan within a minimal budget.

Occupying a space that was formerly a sandwich shop, Vernon's Jerk Paradise contains a 60-seat dining room, small bar, and a new enclosed kitchen where Vernon's Jamaican Jerk Sauce—a special marinade for meat, poultry and fish—is prepared.

The designers chose vinyl floor tiles, drywall partitions with hand-painted murals, and wood lattice and shutters to project the Jamaican design concept within the limited budget.

Size: 1,500 sq. ft.
Budget: $220,000

Interior Designer/Architect
Brennan Beer Gorman Monk/Interiors

Graphic/Lighting Designer
Brennan Beer Gorman Monk/Interiors

Kitchen Designer
AGK Kitcheneering Services

Contractor
Werner Krebs Contracting

Photographer
Anthony T. Alberello

above: **The lounge area is located just off the restaurant entry on an elevated platform.**

above: A creative use of color, decorative sconces, and hand-painted murals lit from recesses in their wall niches enhance the tropical ambience. The wood lattice in the ceiling becomes a decorative and dominant design element.

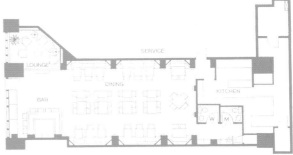

left: Painted by Tromploy, this decorative mural is framed by shutters on both sides. The dark-green upholstery recedes into the mural.

Cafe Japengo

San Diego, California

An Asian-influenced restaurant with a "Pacific Rim" food concept, Cafe Japengo is located in a complex designed by Michael Graves. The melding of two cultures, East and West, and the combination of old and new styles is what gives this restaurant a vital atmosphere.

At the entrance, a large sushi bar and liquor bar are set opposite each other, creating a layout with great energy and excitement. The yin and yang conceptual approach is carried into the other parts of the cafe—the open display kitchen is set against a serene rock garden with punctuations of live bamboo filtering the view to the exterior.

Due to budget considerations, the ceiling and metal joists were left exposed and painted black, providing a sense of greater height. Pebbles in some areas of the floor give textural interest and an "Asian" recall to the design. Private dining areas have black metal partitions with bronze mesh panels. Warm and inviting lighting changes from a high level in the bar areas to a low level in the dining spaces. Color balance is good, and rich, natural wall finishes create a clean contemporary background for furnishings and artwork.

Size: 6,000 sq. ft.
Budget: $112/sq. ft.

above: **Mesh panels create a shimmering form and add to the perceived elegance of this room.**

Interior Designer
Paul Draper and Associates, Inc.

Architects
Paul Draper and Associates, Inc.
Steven Langford Architects

Graphic Designer
David Carter Graphic Design Associates

Lighting Designer
Paul Draper and Associates, Inc.

Kitchen Designer
Thomas Ricca Associates, Inc.

Contractor
Harper Construction

Photographer
Mary McAleer, Milroy/McAleer

right: **An elegant zinc-topped bar is complemented by contemporary stools, and a wait station created from a beautiful piece of Japanese-inspired furniture.**

The black metal support
for the light cables fits
perfectly into the overall
design concept.

right: A charming rock garden lies in the foreground and a "dry river" black pebble detail protects the wall in the dining room.

left: The elegance of "black" as a color statement is shown in Cafe Japengo's dining room.

above: A low, black steel wall divides the two bar areas, and black river pebbles pushed into the stained concrete floor recall a Japanese garden "dry river bed."

Tropica

New York, New York

Tropica is located in midtown Manhattan in the Met Life (formerly Pan Am) Building; this is one of the most central locations one could hope for, as copious numbers of people pass by on their way to and from Grand Central Terminal.

One enters Tropica from the lobby of the office building; the bar area off to the right becomes a "hot spot" just after office hours and hums on through the dinner period. The food concept is Caribbean seafood with a large market selection of fish and seafood.

The designer refers to the interior design concept as a re-creation of a Caribbean great house with the influence of British colonial design elements. He attributes the air of sophistication to the British—their style in colonial architecture is found in the Caribbean.

Gentle arches separate dining areas and highlight the seemingly domestic scale of architectural detailing in these spaces. A large open display kitchen is enhanced by bright, hand-decorated tiles. There is a very open airy feeling about the entire restaurant—it says "Bahamas" loud and clear. The designer used lattice, cove lighting, and tropical murals to further add to the feeling of endless tropical expanse.

Size: 6,250 sq. ft.
Budget: $320/sq. ft.

Interior Designer/Architect
Frederick Brush Design Associates Inc.

Graphic Designer
Alexander Design Associates

Lighting/Kitchen Designer
Frederick Brush Design Associates Inc.

Contractor
Construction by Design

Photographer
Reyndell Stockman

opposite: Varied dining chairs and details at the top of larger columns add to the pleasant Caribbean ambience.

below: With a Caribbean clubby feeling, Tropica's main dining room is richly constructed and decorated.

above: The large open kitchen is enhanced by hand-painted tiles and fresh and exciting food displays.

right: The aqua-marine color of the French doors and the rich woodwork recall the early Colonial era of the Bahamas.

above: The bar has a graphic black and white floor and the beach mural sets the tone of the space. The chairs recall verandahs one might find in the South.

C H A P T E R  4

On the Road

Rasthaus Siegerland Ost

Freudenberg, Germany

This rest stop has self- and full-service food facilities, as well as conference accommodations. The existing building was altered and added to, while differentiating between old and new. Serving as the building's entrance, a new glass tower and dominant staircase element contribute to the spaceship-like, futuristic and streamlined forms of the building.

Fresh food and regional specialties become key elements in the design, as the free-flow servery and partially open kitchen convey the idea of a market with various stands. Off to the sides lie the dining areas. Frosted glass partitions and birch arches give the dining areas just off the servery a particularly warm and intimate atmosphere.

Halogen lighting adds color to the food displays, and makes the space glow.

Size: 8,400 sq. ft.
Budget: $67/sq. ft. (architecture)
$100/sq. ft. (interiors)

Interior Designers
Gabriela Raible, Sabine Vogt, Bernhard Leniger-Salley of Albrecht & Partner

Architect
Claudia Zeilhofer, Albrecht & Partner

Graphic/Lighting Designer
Albrecht & Partner

Kitchen Designer
Albrecht & Partner

Contractor
Gesellschaft für Nebenbetriebe der Bundesautobahnen

Photographer
Wolfgang Pulfer

above: In the evening, lighting projects a warm, inviting welcome to road travelers. The futuristic and streamlined forms project a sense of quality and excitement.

right: Birch-faced plywood forms bring a sophisticated element to the design, which is enhanced by the natural copper, green and brown finishes used. A public dining arcade is located in an alcove beyond this free-flow market.

above: Birch arches define the
space of this dining room,
and the flooring adds a
subtle pattern to the
overall composition.

above: The warm, rich wood
floor, great lighting and
interesting art gives this full-
service dining room an inviting feel and sets it apart from
the other areas within
Rasthaus Siegerland Ost.

below: A small food and drink
bar has frosted glass panels
which are used elsewhere in
the building.

Finely crafted walls and cabinetry are placed so the customer can move freely about them, and wonderful shapes in the ceiling create interesting changes in level. Many walls stop short of the ceilings—some act as screens and dividers, while others take on a more sculptural quality. The materials and finishes are "user-friendly" and easy to maintain.

Rasthaus
Brohltal West

Niederzissen, Germany

The design of this self-service restaurant, located at a service area on the Autobahn in Germany, incorporates a portion of a building from the 1970s. Half of the building was obsolete and had to be demolished, and a dining area with a shop needed to be added. Rasthaus Brohltal West is composed of many elements—a dining room for self-service, free-flow cafeteria, shop, and back-up service spaces for food preparation. Providing natural lighting to the interior spaces, a glass wall "street" emphasizes the connection between old and new. A dominant wall element separates the main dining area from a circular winter garden.

Displays of local fruits, vegetables, cheeses and breads, as well as areas where customers can watch their food being prepared, bring the essence of a "market" to the free-flow servery. The overall feel of this facility is one of excitement, brought in from the major highway just outside.

Size: 6,700 sq. ft.
Budget: $67/sq. ft. (architecture)
$100/sq. ft. (interiors)

Interior Designers
Gabriela Raible, Bernhard Leniger-Salley of
Albrecht & Partner

Architect
Claudia Zeilhofer, Albrecht & Partner

Graphic/Lighting Designer
Albrecht & Partner

Kitchen Designer
Peter Visch, Albrecht & Partner

Contractor
Gesellschaft für Nebenbetriebe der
Bundesautobahnen

Photographer
Bernhard Leniger-Salley, Albrecht & Partner

right: An exciting architectural statement, the building that houses Rasthaus Brohltal West becomes a beacon, a signpost, on the Autobahn.

left: Outside, patrons can enjoy the circular winter garden.

right:
**Specifically
commissioned
for Rasthaus
Brohltal West,
this mural
appears at
the entrance.**

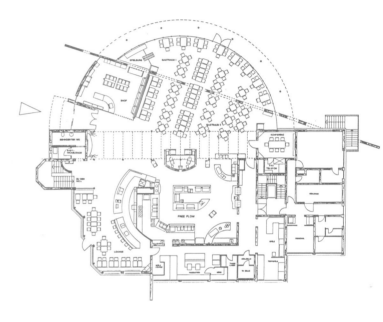

right: The dining room features flexible seating arrangements, from large groupings to tables of two. The crenelated structure in the background is a play lookout tower for children.

Vaterstetten Ost und
Vaterstetten West
Feldkirchen, Germany

The original building of this rest stop was of an odd proportion and had a monotonous character. To solve this problem, an extension was built in the form of an ellipse, with a central steel "tree" construction that is higher than the surrounding roof. A large expanse of windows creates a curved glass facade that faces the street.

The familiar theme of a traditional outside food market in the other rest stops on the Autobahn is the key strategy at Vaterstetten Ost und Vaterstetten West as well. Local produce and made-from-scratch foodstuffs are served, the customer gets involved in the food preparation visually, and there are displays of raw materials in the servery.

Size: 1,550 sq. ft. (extension)
Budget: $67/sq. ft. (architecture)
$100/sq. ft. (interiors)

Interior Designers
Andrea Hilger, Bernhard Leniger-Salley of Albrecht & Partner

Architects
Christine Krebs, Franz Pillat of Albrecht & Partner

Graphic/Lighting Designer
Albrecht & Partner

Kitchen Designer
Peter Visch, Albrecht & Partner

Contractor
Autobahndirektion Südbayern

Photographer
G. u. E. von Voithenberg

above: **Clean, modern and uncomplicated, the reserved exterior contrasts with the fun and exciting marketplace inside.**

below: **Minimal presentation is very effective.**

These stand-up eating tables are eye-catching and unique. Note the glass partition dividing the back bar from the public.

left: The "tree" is the dominant design form in the market-place. Checkerboard floors are a unifying theme throughout.

right: The exposed ducts and hood in the servery add to the marketplace's charm.

Rasthaus
Leipheim
Leipheim, Germany

This rest stop, dating back to the early 1930s, serves fresh, made-from-scratch regional food. Prior to five remodelings, rooms had low ceilings and minimal light and windows. The materials and finishes used are not as high-end as in the other rest stops because this one will have to be demolished in 1997 to accommodate an extension in the highway. Using chipboard, cork and aluminum, the designers created some exciting and provocative designs within a tight budget.

The redesigned and remodeled structure now encompasses a free-flow servery, bar/lounge, dining areas, and a full-service restaurant.

Size: 5,150 sq. ft.
Budget: $60/sq. ft. (architecture)
* $87/sq. ft. (interiors)*

Interior Designers
Gabriela Raible, Sabine Vogt, Bernhard Leniger-Salley of Albrecht & Partner

Architects
Franz Pillat, Klaus Struwe of Albrecht & Partner

Graphic/Lighting Designer
Albrecht & Partner

Kitchen Designer
Peter Visch, Albrecht & Partner

Contractor
Gesellschaft für Nebenbetriebe der Bundesautobahnen

Photographer
Wolfgang Pulfer

right: **A variety of materials interplay with each other and give the banquettes a sculptural quality.**

left: Halogen lighting accentuates the many food displays found throughout the self-service area.

right: Chipboard and aluminum allow for low-budget, but fun designs in this servery.

CHAPTER 5

Hotel Dining

Panorama Restaurant

New World Hotel   Kowloon, Hong Kong

Boasting one of the most spectacular views of Hong Kong's "Fragrant Harbor," the Panorama Restaurant is a seafood grille that puts the dining experience into perspective. A 20-foot-high wall of glass allows an unobstructed view from Kai Tak Airport to Admiralty, while copious food displays highlighting the day's catch, and impressive glass-faced wine cabinets place heavy emphasis on gastronomical delights. The idea behind the design was not to compete with the surroundings, but to complement the patrons with a palette of rich materials and neutral colors. A wave motif, in harmony with the location and theme of the restaurant, laps at the base of buffets and floats overhead on columns. Chairs are dressed in gathered fabric, and intricately patterned mahogany tabletops are set with unconventional place settings and an unusual centerpiece—a live goldfish! Activity of the patrons and artistry of the food presentation are reflected in angled mirrors mounted on the soffits.

Size: 2,700 sq. ft.
Budget: $175/sq. ft.

Interior Designer
DiLeonardo International Inc.

Architect
K.N.W. Architects & Engineers, Ltd.

Graphic/Lighting Designer
DiLeonardo International Inc.

Contractor
Hip Hing Construction Company, Ltd.

Photographer
Arthur Kan Photography

right: Warm, richly stained wood, like in these intricately patterned mahogany-inlay tables and chairs, is a key design element of the restaurant.

right: Fresh displays of the day's catch contribute to the seaside atmosphere of the restaurant.

left: With 20-foot-high windows, the Panorama Restaurant attracts visitors not just for the food, but for the spectacular view of Hong Kong Harbor.

right: An undulating wave pattern adorns buffet fronts and columns.

New World Coffee Shop

New World Hotel   Kowloon, Hong Kong

Located on the fourth floor of the New World Hotel, the New World Coffee Shop serves three meals in a casual, yet sophisticated atmosphere. Food displays and an open grill emphasize "fresh" and "plentiful," and add ambience to the space.

One of the challenges faced by the designers was an obvious circulation path that splits the restaurant's dining spaces and makes the area seem narrow. By eliminating window treat-ments, the dining space is visually widened, and the outdoor courtyard is unified with the whole coffee shop experience.

Warm-colored terra-cotta stone floors and unusual blue and pink lighting fixtures give the interior a light and modern feel while shoji-like window panels add an Oriental touch. Colorful murals complete the design.

Size: 2,400 sq. ft.

Interior Designers
Tom Limone, Chris Cooney,
Robert DiLeonardo of
DiLeonardo International, Inc.

Architect
K.N.W. Architects & Engineers, Ltd.

Graphic Designer
Watermark

Kitchen Designer
U B L

Contractor
Hip Hing Construction Company, Ltd.

Photographer
Arthur Kan Photography

below: **Verdant foliage and terra-cotta floors blend the inside with the outside, visually widening the space.**

A food display, dramatized by lighting and the captivating wall of art behind the banquette, creates interest in this linear dining room.

left: Shoji-like window panels add an Oriental touch, and whimsical wall sconces provide a welcome lift from the utilitarian approach.

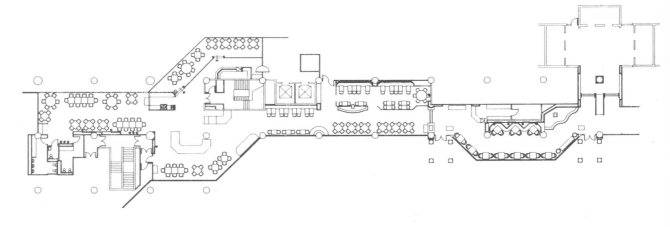

The Catwalk

New World Hotel   Kowloon, Hong Kong

Occupying the former penthouse on the 18th floor of the New World Hotel, The Catwalk has very high ceilings and an upper-level mezzanine (hence the name). A wooden staircase with stainless steel banister, and wall-mounted folds of red and aluminum "wrapping paper" provide entry to both the lower level and catwalk. Enameled steel scrolls in burnished burgundy define the height of the room and contrast with the texture and warmth of the earth-toned checkerboard slate floor.

Four different concepts—a disco, bar, karaoke bar and VIP karaoke rooms—flow together in this space creating a "Texas-Brazilian...salsa...live band" style atmosphere. The customer responds well to this wild but varied mix!

Interior Designer
DiLeonardo International, Inc.

Architect
K.N.W. Architects & Engineers, Ltd.

Contractor
Hip Hing Construction Company, Ltd.

Photographer
Arthur Kan Photography

right: The Catwalk bar has hints of the great American Southwest, with Native American motifs, antler chandeliers, desert colors, rich wood floors, and a back-lit sunburst pattern on the bar face.

left: The double-height space allows views of the interesting curved striped sculpture, harlequin design soffits and steel-topped bar.

Bengawan Solo Indonesian Restaurant

Sahid Jaya Hotel & Tower   Jakarta, Indonesia

Unlike most Indonesian restaurants which tend to mix the region's numerous cuisines together on one menu, this traditional Javanese restaurant serves food exclusively from the city of Solo. Originally hotel storage space, Bengawan Solo has low ceilings and no windows, so the designers chose to focus on special elements created within the restaurant. Traditional serving pieces made from pottery, bamboo, and local woods are displayed in the central serving area, and a large collection of authentic native artifacts gives the restaurant a strong ethnic touch. The entrance, designed as a porte cochere, draws interest with wooden figures of palace guards and a hand-carved gilded frieze. Even the waiters' uniforms are part of the cohesive design concept, and are produced by local craftspeople. A typical Javanese Gamelan orchestra enhances the dining experience.

Size: 4,000 sq. ft.
Budget: $28/sq. ft.

Interior Designer
Atelier 6 Interior

Architect
PRW Arsitek

Graphic Designer
Spectrum

Kitchen Designer
Rotaryana Prima

Contractor
PT. Mataram Maju

Photographer
John Paul Kay

below: **A special porte-cochere design ornamented with traditional figures of palace guards draws attention to the entrance.**

above: **Western-styled seating, the one departure from the traditional theme, illustrates the richness of handmade Javanese fabrics. The handsome parquet flooring is teak and rosewood.**

The central focus of the dining room is the food display and servery. Just behind this area is the Gamelan Orchestra. The artworks are all from the area around the city of Solo.

BENGAWAN SOLO
INDONESIAN RESTAURANT

Restaurant CIII

Washington Square Hotel   New York, New York

Located at 103 Waverly Place in the Washington Square Hotel, Restaurant CIII derives its name from the hotel's address in Roman numerals. The space is 3 feet below sidewalk level with ceilings as low as 7 feet, 9 inches in some places. To bring a certain grandness to this small intimate restaurant, walls are indulged with luminous back-painted glass panels, and horizontal planes are emphasized with wood and fabric treatments. Sound conditioning was a priority for the designers, so several different materials, including gold-silk acoustical ceiling panels, were employed to make the dining room more comfortable. Low-voltage halogen lighting, bounced off ceilings and walls, is very handsome and adds to the richness of the total environment.

American cuisine is the bill of fare in this restaurant, which, as a hotel dining facility, serves every meal period. Specifically designed to boost occupancy rates at the Washington Square Hotel, CIII is quiet yet bustling, elegant yet informal, and intimate yet public.

Size: 1,580 sq. ft.
Budget: $60/sq. ft.

below: **The back-painted glass panels by artist John Jerard are an integral design element. A small percentage of light from bright fluorescents behind the opaque panels is revealed at the edges, creating a sense of depth.**

Interior Designer/Architect
L. Bogdanow & Associates, Architects

Graphic Designer
P. M. Design & Marketing

Lighting/Kitchen Designer
L. Bogdanow & Associates, Architects

Contractor
Hotel Earle Realty Corporation

Photographer
Ross Muir

above: This close-up detail of a
banquette illustrates how the
rich muted tones of rust,
deep-purple and green work
harmoniously together.

Lounge 21

Dai-ichi Hotel Tokyo, Japan

Lounge 21 is located on the top floor of the Dai-ichi Hotel and features a special 180-degree view of downtown Tokyo, including the famed Ginza district. The space of the hotel is long and narrow, so it was not possible to have all areas facing the view through the two-story floor-to-ceiling windows. To solve the problem, the designers decided to create "public" and "private" zones. Intimate private zones are away from the high windows and have lower ceilings, while the more active public spaces have great city views, enhanced by a large mirrored wall.

Featuring a lighter, somewhat casual menu, the restaurant is open for lunch, dinner, and late night cocktails. Both the restaurant and the hotel focus on international as well as domestic markets.

Size: 2,277 sq. ft.

Interior Designer
Media Five Limited

Architect
Mitsubishi Estate Co., Ltd.

Graphic Designers
Ryo Urano, Perry Brewbaker of
Urano Communication Inc.

Lighting Designer
Luminae Souter Lighting Design

Contractor
Shimizu Corporation

Photographer
Luminae Souter Lighting Design

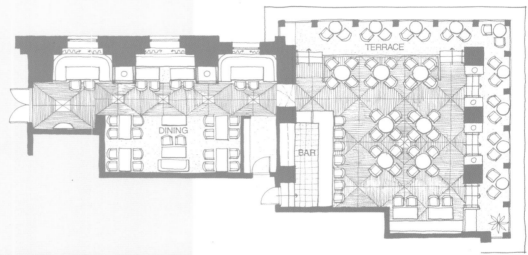

left: **Lounge 21 features a special view of downtown Tokyo through two-story floor-to-ceiling windows.**

left: The lighting does not compete with the view from this 21st-floor aerie, but reveals the warmth of the wood tones in the intricately patterned inlaid floor of the active dining areas.

LOUNGE 21

Trax Cafe Bar

Dai-ichi Hotel Tokyo, Japan

Trax Cafe Bar is a contemporary European cafe where the trendy and au courant crowd gathers for cocktails and light meals. The name "Trax" refers to the famous Shinkansen bullet trains and tracks which can be viewed from floor-to-ceiling windows. The cafe's sleek and streamlined shape allowed for a dynamic and unconventional layout. Matte-black metal railings and a curved bar set a contemporary tone. Hand-painted and textured wall coverings are used on columns and behind the bar, and a subtle black-and-white checked carpet complements the grays and golds of the upholstery. Bright colors found in artwork and accessories are used as accents.

Size: 1,500 sq. ft.

Interior Designer
Media Five Limited

Architect
Mitsubishi Estate Co., Ltd.

Graphic Designer
Ryo Urano, Tracy Tokita of
Urano Communication Inc.

Lighting Designer
Luminae Souter Lighting Design

Contractor
Shimizu Corporation

Photographer
Luminae Souter Lighting Design

below: **Stylized lighting fixtures, whimsical artwork and black-and-white glass artifacts all add an aesthetic commentary to the dramatic interiors.**

left: Although this is a small room, the architects have been able to create the feeling of incredible space. The interesting railing defines the dining and bar areas, and the change in floor levels.

CAFE BAR
TRAX

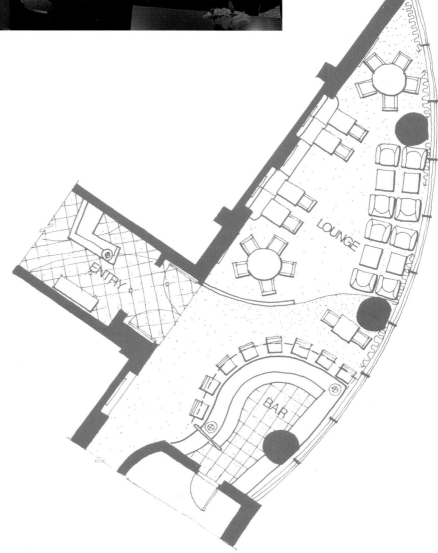

The Royal Abjar Hotel

Dubai, United Arab Emirates

Camel Coffee Shop

Situated in the lobby of the Royal Abjar Hotel, the Camel Coffee Shop is an oasis in the desert. The camel is man's best friend in the region, so this coffee shop is dedicated to these hard working beasts of burden. Metal cutouts of the long-legged creatures are set in front of a 30-foot-long back-lit glass block wall. The space is surrounded by water—long narrow channels, marble clad fountains, connecting pools—every surface evokes "cool and wet" in contrast to the reality just outside. Quatrefoil stainless steel columns rise four stories past pedestrian bridges connecting the floors above, architecturally suggesting a "cathedral-like" space. Palm trees and rattan chairs are part of the leitmotiv, and playful, bold Arabic forms decorate the marble floor. This is not only a place to eat, but a place to rest and relax.

Size: 1,600 sq. ft.

Interior Designers
Stan Glover, Ken Bavaro,
Robert DiLeonardo of
DiLeonardo International, Inc.

Architect
The Fraser Nag Partnership

Graphic Designer
Stan Glover

Lighting Designer
Creative Light Source

Kitchen Designer
Cini Little

Contractor
Almulla Construction Co. (Pvt) Ltd.

Photographer
Robert Miller

right: A massive glass block wall creates a cool textured backdrop for the metal camel figures, and the rattan chairs suggest the comfort of an oasis in the desert environment.

above: **Behind a dessert buffet, the glass block wall is lit with cool and soothing blue neon.**

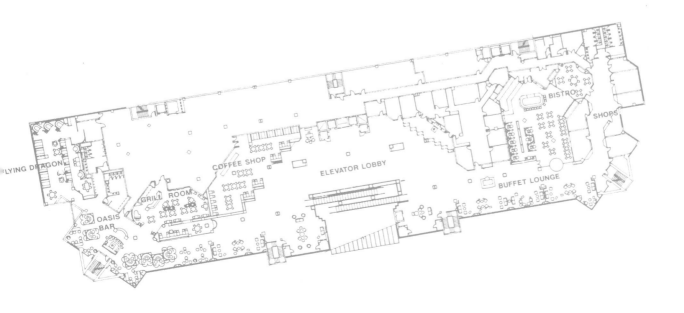

FLYING DRAGON

COFFEE SHOP

ELEVATOR LOBBY

BISTRO

SHOPS

GRILL ROOM

BUFFET LOUNGE

OASIS BAR

The Oasis Lounge Bar

To achieve a traditional Arabic theme in The Oasis Lounge Bar, the designers used bedouin tents to create private and semi-private areas where patrons can enjoy drinks and conversation. Acting as elegant canopies, these tents create a vivid design. Pools of running water provide a soothing environment where 70 can sit in comfort. Modern chairs and sofas add an extra Western touch.

left: Elegant bedouin tents are the most striking element in this lounge. The area looks out to the hotel lobby and other food and bar units.

Flying Dragons

This 95-seat restaurant is unmistakably influenced by the East with its shoji screens at the entrance, and two huge dragons flying across the ceiling. Rich wood, black lacquer furniture and turquoise and rose upholstery used throughout the restaurant add to the serene ambience.

right: Brass torchieres uplight the ceiling and provide indirect lighting for the dining patrons.

The Bistro

The Bistro, a modern version of a French cafe, has steel chairs and high-tech touches which contribute to an upbeat mood. A 3-meter salt water aquarium, adjacent to the restaurant, houses living coral and all sorts of tropical fish. "Shark's teeth" are suspended from the ceiling and set into the floor. From the bar, an exhibition kitchen is visible. The main restaurant seats one hundred diners, and a small private dining area can be screened off to comfortably seat 22 patrons.

left: **An arbor device covering seating areas adjacent to the main bar is draped with banners. Strong color accents the tables.**

C H A P T E R  **6**

Continental Cafés

Papa Razzi

Cambridge, Massachusetts

Yes, Papa Razzi is Italian! Northern Italian to be specific. Located in the CambridgeSide Galleria and attracting customers from the mall, nearby theaters and local neighborhoods, the restaurant is designed to emphasize people-watching opportunities. Food preparation in the large open kitchen with its wood burning oven becomes part of the "show," and the imposing, highly detailed mahogany bar makes its presence known, serving lunch during the day and drinks in the evening.

Hinting at what happens inside, the exterior has large colorful awnings with overscaled canned goods label designs that lead into a space of controlled casualness. The rear wall is covered with Italian posters of American movies, and photos of famous personalities in casual situations. Columns have custom painted artwork, and the floor shows 19th-century tile patterns and colors. Crisp white tablecloths contrast with casual blackboard menus, giving further vent to the nostalgia suggested here. Italian music, from popular to opera, completes the mood.

Size: 7,500 sq. ft.
Budget: $500,000

Interior Designers
Morris Nathanson, David Jackson,
Peter A. Niemitz of
Morris Nathanson Design

Architect
Arris Design

Graphic/Kitchen Designer
Back Bay Restaurant Group

Lighting Designer
Morris Nathanson Design

Contractor
Northern Construction

Photographer
Ron Manville

above: **Due to local signage limitations, awnings, combined with neon letters, became the restaurant's only exterior identification.**

below: **White tablecloths, contrasted with dark wood floors, give the space a certain elegance and class.**

left: Mahogany wood adds warmth to the traditional bar. Overhead, illuminated graphic panels draw visual interest.

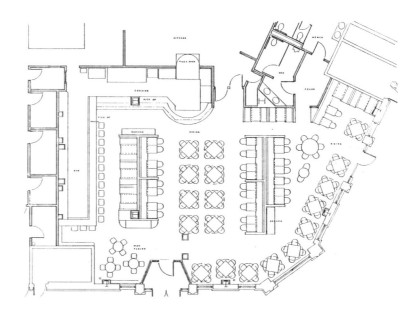

right: Walls covered with Italian posters and candid celebrity photographs are highlighted with theatrical spots.

below: An open kitchen is an important feature in the design. Tops of structural columns are decorated with custom artwork.

The *Cheesecake Factory*

Newport Beach, California

The Cheesecake Factory, a full-service restaurant with a moderately priced menu, serves a variety of foods to a wide range of customers. It was a big risk for The Cheesecake Factory to take this space, because it was formerly occupied by a very upscale restaurant that did not succeed. Overcoming the challenge, the designers improved visibility and access to the establishment by incorporating a second entrance. Storefronts were also added to give the restaurant its own identity.

Inside, Egyptian tulip-figured capitals top decorative columns, and murals create mesmerizing scenes on the ceiling. Limestone, used for flooring and tabletops, is enriched by deeply toned cherry wood and glazed wall finishes nearby. Custom designed lighting fixtures are used throughout and traditional French bistro chairs and touches of copper impart a casual flair. A semi-open exhibition kitchen is partially screened from view by a large expanse of booths and etched glass. A take-out bakery is adjacent to the new entrance.

Size: 9,583 sq. ft.

Interior Designer
Hatch Design Group

Lighting/Kitchen Designer
Hatch Design Group

Contractor
Pacific Southwest Development
(PSD)

Photographer
Deidra Davidson

below: **The entrance has a visually captivating ceiling mural and a patterned limestone floor. Off to the right is the take-out and bakery.**

above: **Colorful hand-painted wall surfaces and etched glass panels add interest to these intimate booths.**

right: **Brass accents, like the stair banister, and custom lighting fixtures reveal the high level of design.**

below: **Decorative columns are topped with Egyptian tulip-figured capitals.**

left: **The view of the Pacific Ocean out of the front windows is an added attraction to The Cheesecake Factory.**

Brio

New York, New York

Brio is a small Italian bistro in midtown Manhattan, adjacent to the "hot" shopping areas. With all the warmth and coziness of an intimate European library, this bistro has custom-designed architectural metalwork that holds magazines and newspapers, and antique porcelain pulley lamps. Custom wine racks situated at the rear of the dining room give the wall both beauty and texture, while wood paneling and a detailed wood ceiling bring in warmth. All walls are created using different decorative elements, making the small dining area multidimensional.

Interior Designers
Tony Chi, Albert Chen of
Tony Chi & Associates

Contractor
Harry Molina Furniture Co.

Photographer
Dub Rogers

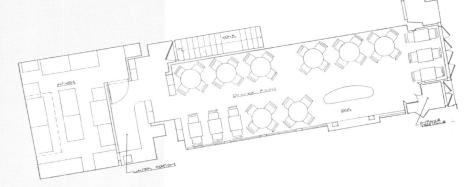

opposite: **Brio is a great place to catch up on reading while dining in a library-like atmosphere.**

below: **Brio's exterior is very inviting; the space is quite small, and one can view the entire restaurant from the street.**

134

French cafe chairs are decorative and comfortable.

below: **Warm-toned wood, brass metalwork and terra-cotta floor tiles add to the coziness of the room, and a coffered ceiling helps control the noise.**

Crêpe à la Carte

Washington, D. C.

Crêpe à la Carte serves French fast food during business hours, then converts to a more casual French cafe during off-peak hours. The menu ranges from crepes, sandwiches, soups and salads to quiche and desserts.

Being extremely small at only 500 square feet, the space is visually doubled by an angled mirrored wall. A ceiling vault, indirectly lit by a continuous light cove and painted with a mural of sky and clouds, adds to the illusion of an enlarged and airy space. Cabinets and unique menu boards are natural cherry wood, and counters and tabletops are marble. The floor has a graphic black-and-white checkerboard pattern. This fun design has lots of personality and impact.

Size: 500 sq. ft.
Budget: $300/sq. ft.

Interior Designer/Architect
Valerio Simini, Architect
(formerly of Brock Simini, Architects)

Lighting/Kitchen Designer
Valerio Simini, Architect

Contractor
Dan Halpern
(formerly of Imago, Inc.)

Photographer
Dennis Kan

right: Unique, and rather formal cherry-wood menu boards are mounted on pilasters.

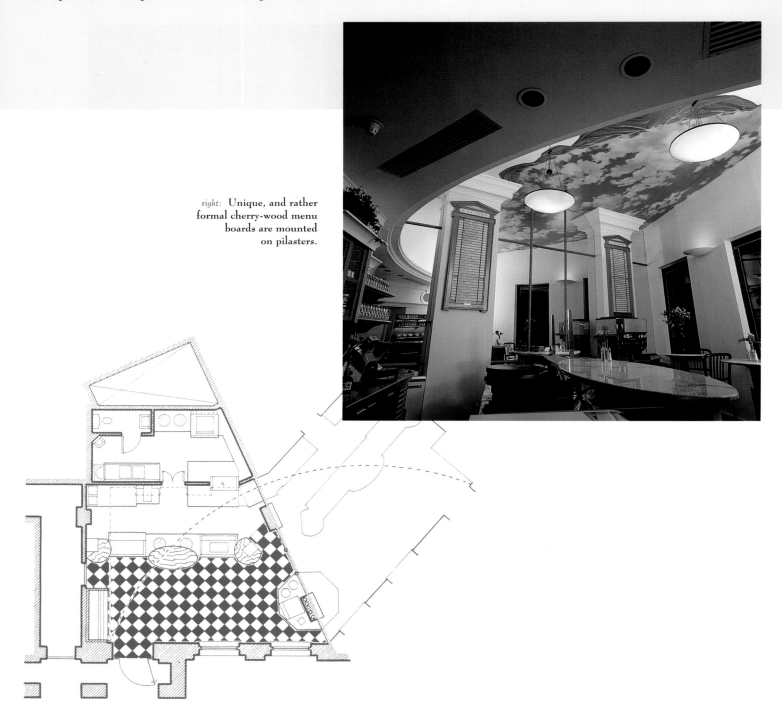

above: Mirrors and trompe l'oeil painting are cleverly used to make a small space seem grand.

left: Ceiling details, molding and woodwork add an exciting, unexpected richness.

Pomodoro/Marabella

Philadelphia, Pennsylvania

Pomodoro/Marabella is a contemporary Northern Italian restaurant located in the heart of Philadelphia's City Center. The restaurant occupies space that was "left-over" following the construction of a mezzanine office space. The resulting low ceiling over most of the restaurant presented a particular design challenge. To achieve volume, the designers created a vaulted ceiling in the high space along the window dining section. In the low-ceilinged areas, they used floating abstract planes to provide relief, achieving an attractive sculptural effect.

Pomodoro Marabella's 7,000 square feet of space includes an open kitchen that serves antipasto, salads and desserts. The food display is an important design asset in this restaurant that caters to young sophisticated diners. Subtle lighting, dramatic color and the use of natural materials throughout contribute to the restaurant's pleasant ambience.

Size: 7,000 sq. ft.
Budget: $200/sq. ft.

Interior Designer/Architect
SRK Architects

Lighting Designer
Tigue Lighting

Kitchen Designer
Marstan Industries, Inc.

Contractor
Gaudet Associates

Photographer
Matt Wargo

below: **Changes of level give relief to a low ceiling, and cables for low-voltage lighting add interest.**

above: This dining area has its own special character. Displayed within the bins on the two walls is a special collection of wines and related paraphernalia.

The open kitchen is like a
still life; beautiful food compositions are a major part of
the action here. The black
shelving on the rear wall sets
off the ingredients in an
almost boutique-like idiom.

left: The highest space in the restaurant is located along the window wall. Here the designers have created a vaulted ceiling and playful, elegant lighting.

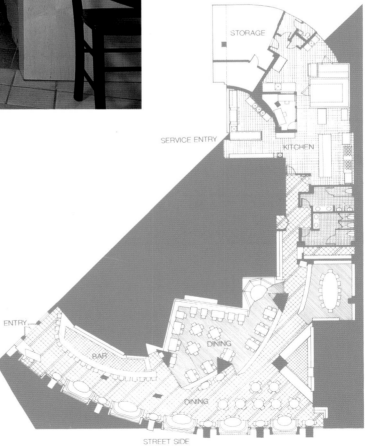

Caffe Angelica

Garden City Park,   New York

Caffe Angelica caters to young suburban professionals, and serves moderately priced items such as pasta, grilled dishes and brick oven pizza. Constructed off-site and trucked to its present location, this prefabricated restaurant is square in structure with a central atrium and an open kitchen that acts as the focal point for the dining space.

The walls are painted a faux finish, and the soffits in the atrium are covered with references to Tuscan ruins. Terra-cotta tiled floors are decorated with blue and white inlays and tabletops are pink/gray polished granite. The chairs recall French cafe chairs one might find on Boulevard Saint Germaine in Paris.

Size: 3,240 sq. ft.
Budget: $200/sq. ft.

Interior Designer
Lori Freesmeier & Associates Inc.

Architect/Contractor
DeRaffle Manufacturing Inc.

Kitchen Designer
AJM Associates, Inc.

Photographer
Scott Rothstein

below: **The atrium ceiling has been raised, leaving lower ceilings around the perimeter for an intimate dining experience.**

left: Faux-finished walls and dark stained wood provide a nice foil for black-and-white woven French cafe chairs.

right: Natural light filters through the bar shelving, creating a jewel-like effect. The granite bar top matches the tabletops.

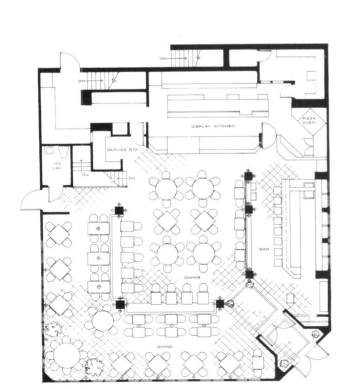

Sfuzzi
Scottsdale, Arizona

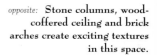

opposite: Stone columns, wood-coffered ceiling and brick arches create exciting textures in this space.

Sfuzzi means "fun food" in Italian slang, according to its owners, and "fun" can be seen in the facade of this restaurant, which is a crazy combination of Spanish Mission and Italian Country with touches of Americana.

A contemporary restaurant inside a historic building, Sfuzzi has brick arches and walls with painted Italianate frescos. The roof has been raised, creating ceilings as high as 22 feet, and the resulting spatial volume is filled with natural light from skylights and windows.

Elegant wood-coffered ceilings are supported by adoquin stone columns and floors are terracotta tile. The lighting is simple and contemporary, with a low-voltage cable system, iron chandeliers and pendant fixtures, and is meant to appear as a retrofit in a building that did not originally accommodate electricity.

An open kitchen was created to lend energy to the room, and an exterior courtyard was made from previously interior space.

Size: 4,966 sq. ft.

Interior Designer
Paul Draper and Associates, Inc.

Architects
Paul Draper and Associates, Inc.
John E. Wheeler Architects

Graphic Designer
David Carter Graphic Design Associates

Lighting Designer
Paul Draper and Associates, Inc.

Kitchen Designer
Food Service Concepts

Contractor
Deneuve Construction

Photographer
A. F. Payne Photographic

below: Sfuzzi's exterior architecture combines Spanish Mission and Italian Country styles with a touch of Americana.

left: This ceiling has wood staves laid between massive oak beams. An antique fireplace and mantel adds sculptural interest.

Sfuzzi

San Diego, California

A circa 1910 brick and stucco building in the "Gas Light" district of downtown San Diego turned out to be the perfect space to express the Sfuzzi concept of putting a contemporary restaurant inside an older building. Brick walls have the built-up patina of natural aging, and layers of texture reveal the various changes the structure has undergone through the years.

Exposed wood trusses were lightly sandblasted to make the wood warmer and more textured, and oak plank floors are outlined by green European slate. The 25-foot space is flooded with natural light coming in through skylights and 18-foot-high windows.

As in other Sfuzzi restaurants, exposed brick walls have applications of painted Italianate frescos and trompe l'oeil. The open kitchen is largely ceramic and hand-glazed terra-cotta tile. The majority of the lighting employs a low-voltage, cable-hung system imported from Holland.

size: 5,523 sq. ft.

Interior Designer
Paul Draper and Associates, Inc.

Architects
Paul Draper and Associates, Inc.
John E. Wheeler Architects

Graphic Designer
David Carter Graphic Design Associates

Kitchen Designer
Food Service Concepts

Contractor
BTS Construction

Photographer
Glenn Cormier

left: The interior brick arches bear Italianate frescos, further adding to the perception of "old and uncovered."

left: The majority of the lighting employs a low-voltage, cable-hung system. Shown here, the open kitchen is reminiscent of Italy.

right: **Sfuzzi's exterior invites prospective customers with its cafe appeal and overhead awnings.**

Sfuzzi

Union Station, Washington, D.C.

Occupying two levels of the Union Station building in Washington, D.C., this Sfuzzi is one of the largest most upscale restaurants in the chain. Another great example of a contemporary Italian restaurant placed within the confines of an antique structure, Sfuzzi, Washington, D.C. affords views of the Capitol Building and of the station's great barrel vaulting.

One challenge confronted by the designers was a newly constructed mezzanine which separated the original room into two distinct spaces, and destroyed the architectural integrity of the historical space. To solve the problem, cutouts in the mezzanine open each level to each other, so a constant exchange of energy makes the space very fluid and exciting. Bridges and stairs help to unify these two spaces further. The architectural treatments of the mezzanine and stairs are deliberately contemporary, allowing the historical aspects of Union Station to be viewed as one space.

A small open kitchen serves the high-energy bar on the main level of the restaurant, and a second smaller bar serves the mezzanine.

Interior Designer
Paul Draper and Associates, Inc.

Architects
Paul Draper and Associates, Inc.
Studio II Architects

Graphic Designer
David Carter Graphic Design Associates

Lighting Designer
Paul Draper and Associates, Inc.

Kitchen Designer
Food Service Concepts

Contractor
Edmar Construction

Photographer
Walter Smalling

below: **Barrel vaults, bridges connecting various dining spaces, and the lavish use of oak planking on the floors are apparent in this view of Sfuzzi.**

The staircase to the mezzanine is ceremonial and very contemporary in design—a nice contrast to the classical order of architecture that exists in Union Station.

CHAPTER

All-American

The Great American Cafe

Glastonbury, Connecticut

The Great American Cafe is just that, great, in the sense that 16 themed dining rooms representing different "slices of America" are brought together all under one roof! This full-service restaurant of regional American cuisine is a grand tour of the country. From a Maine cabin replete with logs, to a New York City delicatessen, there are so many choices, it's tough to decide where to dine. An open kitchen, located in the delicatessen, helps give the area that "New York intensity" through all the hustle and bustle. Lots of surprises in these dining rooms make The Great American Cafe a special and unique place to visit.

The multistory building, originally designed by Robert Stern, turned out to be an especially difficult piece of architecture to work with in terms of this project. Large expanses of windows, at first seen as problems, were made into a positive design element. Window treatments were made to architecturally and decoratively fit the particular room they were in, without affecting the exterior view, thus respecting the architect's original design.

Size: 7,266 sq. ft. (restaurant area only)

Interior Designer/Architect
Frederick Brush Design Associates, Inc.

Graphic/Lighting Designer
Frederick Brush Design Associates, Inc.

Kitchen Designer
S.E. Rykoff and Company

Contractor
Louis Wade Construction

Photographer
Reyndell Stockman

opposite: An old-fashioned Midwestern ice cream parlor has a pressed tin ceiling, fans and period lighting.

left: An all-American detail from one of the dining rooms is just one of many surprises that make this cafe a unique place to visit.

right: An old Southwestern gas station comes complete with a squeaky screen door and real gas pumps.

left: The shell of the building, with its large expanse of windows, was designed by Robert Stern.

right: A portion of the open kitchen appears behind this unusual 1950s-themed New York deli.

right: **The ceiling of the Chesapeake Bay Area dining room is treated with various buoys.**

A cajun shack room filled
with strings of hot peppers is
lined with shelves of tabasco
bottles.

North Street Grill

Great Neck, New York

Brendan Walsh is the chef and part owner of the North Street Grill, a casual yet elegant 1990s-style tavern located on Long Island's "Gold Coast." Creatively prepared, the food is regional American, and its quality relates to the design quality of the restaurant. The designers created a large and exciting gathering place that encourages people-watching and socializing. Changes in floor level and horseshoe-shaped upholstered booths pull the space into more intimate seating arrangements, and help bring the scale of the room down to human size.

Wooden trusses add unexpected excitement and elegance to the large space. In full view of the main raised platform, the entire rear wall features an open kitchen with a wood burning stove that becomes the focus of this restaurant during dining hours. Stained glass custom lighting fixtures are whimsical and fun, and the colorful, up-to-date fabrics on the booths add interest and warmth.

Size: 10,000 sq. ft.
Budget: $900,000

Interior Designer
Peter A. Niemitz,
Morris Nathanson Design

Architect
Erwin Ladau, AIA

Graphic Designer
Adkins Balchunas

Lighting Designer
Morris Nathanson Design

Contractor
Sullivan & McGrath Construction

Photographer
Ron Manville Photography

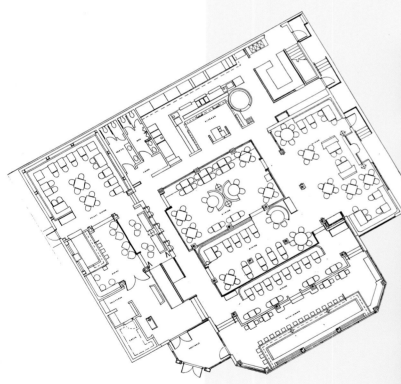

right: **Decorative fabrics on banquettes and booths work well together and with the stained glass lighting fixtures.**

left: Tile color and pattern give the bar personality, charm and durability. Old-fashioned bar stools add a cozy touch.

right: Graphics, lighting and architectural elements create a stylish exterior.

left: The open kitchen is handsome yet utilitarian. A wood burning, freestanding brick oven with wood storage below is set and ready for action.

**Banquettes and booths
are decorated with patterned
fabric, breaking up the large
space.**

above: Changes in dining platform heights promote easy viewing throughout.

Metro Diner II

Tulsa, Okla.

Metro Diner II recalls 1950s roadside diners like those found along Route 66. Traditional diner food, such as chicken-fried steaks, classic barbecue, milk shakes and french fries is served.

The diner is divided into three different areas. The main dining room in the center has a raised seating platform against a glass wall. Above this area is a second-floor stage set with period furniture where local talent performs. The second dining room has a car theme and is decorated with car posters and hubcap lighting fixtures. It can be separated from the other areas by an overhead garage door. A private Western-themed room provides the third dining area, and it has vintage memorabilia, stuffed animal trophies, wagon wheel chandeliers, and of course Western art. There is also a gift shop where customers may purchase hula hoops and X-ray glasses.

Lighting throughout the diner is a mix of recessed downlights, track lighting, and vintage 1950s fixtures. Neon signs are also used in the various dining rooms.

Size: 6,000 sq. ft.

Interior Designers
Kent David Oellien, Craig A. Hime, ASID,
Rick L. Bartholomew, ASID of
Synar•Oellien Design Associates, Inc.

Architect
Stephen J. Olsen, AIA,
Olsen-Coffey Architects

Graphic/Lighting Designer
Randy Frederick,
Frederick Sommers & Western

Kitchen Designer
Roby-Jeremiah-Associates

Contractor
Buck Construction Company

Photographer
Reyndell Stockman

right: **Metro II reflects 1950s American culture with its backseat-style booths and use of paint colors and vinyls of that era.**

left: A large window allows a view into the kitchen's activity, furthering the feel of a busy roadside diner.

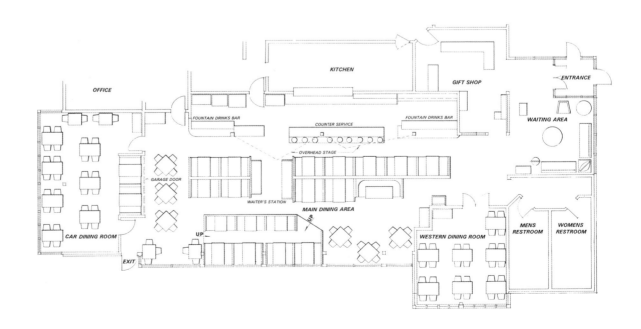

The stage, which often showcases local talent, is an important element at Metro Diner II. Classic examples of 1950s furniture are used as props.

right: The waiting area opens on to the gift shop and fountain drink area where pop billboard art adds to the catching ambience.

below: Period signs, a classic kitchen pick-up window, and "sunburst" stainless steel panels bring back an old-time diner feel.

The main dining room features a
raised seating area where customers
are entertained by live performers.
An original '50s television plays
famous '50s TV shows.

801 Steak & Chop House

Des Moines, Iowa

Located on the mezzanine of the tallest building in the state of Iowa, 801 Steak & Chop House serves traditional steak-house fare, as well as seafood and pasta. The client wanted to create a "showcase" establishment that would rival the private clubs in Des Moines, and the result is a public restaurant that is somewhat upscale in feeling. The American steak houses of the 1920s were the inspiration for the atmosphere created here, which was then given an updated flair. Double-paned sandblasted glass appears on booths, in private dining areas, and on the front door. Tables and booth partitions are made of cherry wood, and floors are oak with marble and stained-wood inlays. Deep hunter-green is the primary color used, and livestock art displayed throughout the restaurant interior underscores the steak house theme. Patrons must walk past the open kitchen to be seated. This adds authenticity to the feel of the restaurant and confidence in the food quality and preparation.

Special attention to the restaurant's print collateral. Wine lists, menus—even matchboxes are all beautifully designed and orchestrated.

Size: 5,800 sq. ft.

Interior/Graphic Designer
Sayles Graphic Design

Architect
Environmental Design Group, Ltd.

Kitchen Designer
Bolton & Hay, Inc.

Photographer
Bill Nellans Photography

above: The packaging of take-out bags is in keeping with the total visual identity of the restaurant.

left: Decorative concepts, like the wood inlay floor of this private dining room, are carried through all the spaces.

left: Booth and table seatings are available in the main dining room. The velvet draperies of two smaller, semi-private dining areas can be drawn for additional privacy.

below: High-backed booths with etched glass panels create an intimate dining space.

Hi-Life
Restaurant & Bar

New York, New York

Hi-Life Restaurant & Bar is a throwback to the glamourous nightclubs that lined the streets of New York City in the '40s. Anchoring the corner of 72nd Street and First Avenue, this restaurant is rich with allusions to clubs past. Art Deco elements like shiny black enamel and chrome moldings grace the exterior, and a giant aquarium filled with exotic fish is at the entrance. Curvaceous stainless steel rails and semi-circular booths, reminiscent of Ginger Rogers and Fred Astair films, give the space movement.

A cocktail lounge, tucked away in the back of the restaurant, reminds one of the "speakeasys" of Harlem. Heavy red drapes with a playing card design separate the lounge from the restaurant, providing patrons with a more intimate place to dine and talk. In addition to serving a mixed grilled, American eclectic menu, Hi-Life features a sushi bar.

A screen of poker-playing dogs, tufted green-leather walls, black-and-white photographs and circular mirrors also help to re-create the mood and ambience of 1940s nightclubs in Hi-Life Restaurant & Bar.

Size: 3,500 sq. ft.
Budget: $50,000

Interior Designers
David Rockwell, Jay Haverson
Richard Truemner,
Carol DiCicco Vinci of
Haverson/Rockwell Architects P. C.

Architect/Lighting Designer
Haverson/Rockwell Architects P. C.

Graphic Designer
Head Productions

Kitchen Designer
Eric Bromberg

Contractors
Wave Dancer (interior)
Tara Store Front (exterior)

Photographer
Paul Warchol Photography

below: **The patterned drapery that defines this backroom space is reminiscent of the "speakeasys" of 1940s Harlem.**

above: **The spirit of Hi-Life is evident in its Art Deco design elements.**

left: **A line of semi-circular booths creates a serpentine form, bringing movement to the space.**

Bugaboo Creek

Warwick, Rhode Island

Bugaboo Creek is a theme restaurant that says "mountains!" loud and clear. Inspired by the Rocky Mountains and the great hunting lodges of the American Northwest, the design incorporates materials and artifacts found in that region. Knotty pine walls and wood floors set the tone. Antler chandeliers, artifacts and artwork add to the ambience while open fireplaces and the smell of burning wood complete the mood.

The food concept works well with the design—affordable steaks are enjoyed by young and old alike in Bugaboo's relaxed atmosphere. It's a fun, memorable place to brings the kids. Animetronic figures, programmed to speak every minute or two, are an added attraction.

Because this restaurant is located in a space that had already housed a number of restaurant ventures prior to Bugaboo Creek, the designers felt that a unique and different look was needed. They completely renewed the exterior, outside signage and landscaping. For budget considerations, many interior features were retained.

Size: 7,000 sq. ft.
Budget: $550,000

Interior Designer
Peter A. Niemitz,
Morris Nathanson Design

Architect
Arris Design

Graphic Designer
Idea Graphics

Lighting Designer
Morris Nathanson Design

Kitchen Designer
Paramount Restaurant Supply

Contractor
Shawmut Design & Construction

Photographer
Warren Jagger Photography, Inc.

opposite: **The hunting lodge theme is evident throughout Bugaboo Creek, from its knotty pine walls and wood floors to its antler chandeliers.**

left: **The restaurant's unique exterior was completely renewed with a Rocky Mountain appeal.**

right: **A memorable place to visit, Bugaboo Creek is decorated with artifacts found in the American Northwest.**

Googie's

New York, New York

new twist to traditional Greek diners, Googie's is an upscale Italian diner geared to attract an Upper East Side clientele. The ambience is light and airy, with sparkling steel accents, a natural stone floor, and polished granite surfaces on areas that get a lot of wear. High-gloss laminated ceiling coffers and mirrors on walls and columns visually enlarge the space. Monopoint low-voltage spots and custom-designed pendant fixtures produce lighting that is bright and decorative with a 1950s feel. The existing kitchen was retained to hold down costs, and its traditional diner pass-through window reinforces customers' awareness of fresh food preparation.

Size: 3,500-4,000 sq. ft.
Budget: $125/sq. ft.

below: **The seat backs of the traditional diner booths have a '50s design motif.**

Interior Designers
Morris Nathanson, David Jackson
Peter A. Niemitz of
Morris Nathanson Design

Architect
David Turner Architects

Lighting Designer
Morris Nathanson Design

Kitchen Designer
Howard Pascoe

Contractor
C.J. Construction

Photographer
Peter Paige Associates, Inc.

above: **Bright lighting enhances reflective surfaces.**

left: **Vaulted ceilings with sparkling metal details and '50s-style chairs recall diners of the old days.**

left: Colorful materials, reflective surfaces and bright lighting make the space light and airy.

below: Mirrored panels visually broaden the narrow space.

Silver Diner

Towson, Maryland

The Silver Diner at Towson Town Center is the largest of four Silver Diners built to date, seating more than 200 people in 6,500 square feet of space. Adapting the prototype diner to a shopping center location was a major design challenge. Located at the base of a 52-foot-high wall, the diner successfully holds its own ground in the massive fortress of the Towson Center. A beacon to passersby, the building itself acts as a sign—a concept that is reinforced by the highly polished stainless steel, black-and-white checkerboard pattern, and neon clock tower with its motto "It's Time to Dine."

Durable and easily maintained materials and finishes were chosen to emphasize the design features of this updated classic American diner. The polished stainless steel with its intricate sunburst pattern is especially noteworthy along with the pink Formica in classic "Boomerang" pattern. Careful attention was given to signage and lighting, which combines neon, incandescent, and halogen downlights.

Silver Diner is a "democratic" American eating place enjoyed by all types of people. The atmosphere and food experience make it a comfortable home away from home.

Size: 6,500 sq. ft.

Interior Designer
Charles Morris Mount, Inc.

Architect
James L. Brown and Associates

Graphic/Lighting Designer
Charles Morris Mount, Inc.

Kitchen Designer
Cini Little International

Contractor
Uniwest Inc.

Photographer
Doug Brown

above: **With tremendous graphic visual appeal, Silver Diner holds its own against a 52-foot-high concrete wall.**

left: **A patterned tile floor and modern food display cases welcome customers just inside the entrance.**

right: A small, linear dining room with a skylight grafted onto the exterior wall of the shopping center, is the signature structure of the Silver Diner chain.

left: Touches of a classic American diner, like this jukebox, are found throughout Silver Diner.

Formica brand "Boomerang" and "Linen" pattern plastic laminate, and highly-polished countertops give The Silver Diner an old-time diner feel.

The Good Diner

New York, New York

Located at the corner of 42nd Street and 11th Avenue, The Good Diner is unlike any other diner. It is not a reproduction of a 1940s-style diner—there's almost nothing "retro" about it. The design uses everyday materials in a fresh, innovative way.

Two large volumes comprise this space. The front room is designed for counter service and has booths that overlook 42nd Street. A more flexible seating arrangement is offered in the back. Handrails between the two spaces spell out *GOOD*.

Playful elements are used in both the interior and graphic design. Stools and banquettes are upholstered with Naugahyde in bright primary colors, and floors and tabletops are covered with three types of linoleum. The restaurant's logo pictures a halo-topped coffee cup, and this image extends throughout to the menus, signage and other collateral.

Size: 3,000 sq. ft.
Budget: $45/sq. ft.

Interior Designer/Architect
James Biber, Pentagram

Graphic Designer
Michael Bierut, Pentagram

Lighting Designer
Pentagram

Kitchen Designer/Contractor
Gotham Equities

Photographer
Reven T. C. Wurman

left: The menu cover illustrates the coffee cup topped with its halo.

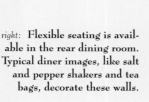

right: Flexible seating is available in the rear dining room. Typical diner images, like salt and pepper shakers and tea bags, decorate these walls.

above: Hanging glass fixtures over the booths are shown in this view of the main dining room from 42nd Street.

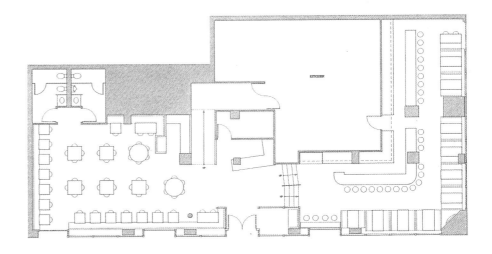

left: The handrails between the two dining areas actually spell out *GOOD*.

right: The Good Diner's playful logo pops up throughout the restaurant—even in the floor.

right: The graphic and color concept is carried through in printed materials, as seen in this matchbook design.

below: Naugahyde stools in vibrant primary colors contrast nicely with the linoleum counters.

Rayz

Cambridge, Massachusetts

Rayz is a casual Floridian restaurant with a Gulf Coast flavor featuring the food and atmosphere of a roadside crabhouse. Weathered colors, lots of fun antique signage and a casual flow make up the atmosphere of Rayz. Multi-colored chairs and booths, worn patinated finishes and eccentric ceiling details all contribute to the homey, friendly Southern ambience.

Food is prepared in an open kitchen, reinforcing the Gulf Coast crabhouse theme, where everything is a show and happens in full view. The bar-in-the-round has a tropical look and allows for easy conversation among the mainly college student clientele.

Interior Designers
Blase Gallo, David Jackson,
Morris Nathanson of
Morris Nathanson Design

Architect
Arris Design

Graphic/Kitchen Designer
Back Bay Restaurant Group

Lighting Designer
Morris Nathanson Design

Contractor
Northern Construction

Photographer
Ron Manville Photography

left: **The exterior signage introduces Rayz as a fun and playful place.**

below: **Multi-colored chairs and booths and fun antique signage make up the atmosphere of Rayz.**

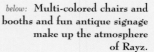

above: Eccentric ceiling details contribute to the homey Southern ambience.

right: The atmosphere of a roadside crabhouse is completely conveyed in Rayz interior design elements.

above: The Gulf Coast crab-house theme where everything is a show and happens in the open is reinforced in the open kitchen.

left: Terra-cotta floor tiles and differently colored stained woods add to the fun atmosphere of Rayz.

above: Expanded wire mesh
used over a deep-turquoise
stained wood bar is high-tech,
fun and memorable.

APPENDIX

801 Steak & Chop House
801 Grand Avenue
Des Moines, IA 50309

Anzu
4620 McKinney Avenue
Dallas, TX 75205

Baldini's Restaurant
5 Stockwell Drive
Avon, MA 02332

Bank of America Cafeteria
1825 East Buckeye Road
Phoenix, AZ 85034

**Bengawan Solo
Indonesian Restaurant**
Sahid Jaya Hotel & Tower
Jl. Jend. Sudirman 86
Jakarta 10220 Indonesia

The Bistro
The Royal Abjar Hotel
PO Box 8668
Dubai, United Arab Emirates

Bitu
Schönleinsplatz 4
D-8600 Bamberg, Germany

Brio
786 Lexington Avenue
New York, NY 10021

Bugaboo Creek
30 Jefferson Boulevard
Warwick, RI 02888

Cafe Briacco
125 High Street
Boston, MA 02110

Café Japengo
8960 University Center Lane
San Diego, CA 92122

Caffe Angelica
2370 Jericho Turnpike
Garden City, NY 11040

The Camel Coffee Shop
The Royal Abjar Hotel
PO Box 8668
Dubai, United Arab Emirates

The Catwalk
New World Hotel
22 Salisbury Road
Tsimshatsui Kowloon, Hong Kong

The Cheesecake Factory
1141 Newport Center Drive
Newport Beach, CA 92660

Crêpe à la Carte
1304 18th Street, NW
Washington, DC 20036

Dino's Cafe
La Jolla Center, Tower 1
4660 La Jolla Village Drive
La Jolla, CA 92121

Fama
1416 Fourth Street
Santa Monica, CA 90401

Felissimo Tearoom
10 West 56th Street
New York, NY 10019

Flying Dragons
The Royal Abjar Hotel
PO Box 8668
Dubai, United Arab Emirates

The Good Diner
554 11th Avenue
New York, NY 10018

Googie's
1491 Second Avenue
New York, NY 10021

The Great American Cafe
Somerset Square
Glastonbury, CT 06033

Hi-Life Restaurant & Bar
1340 First Avenue
New York, NY 10021

Kachina Grill
330 Hope Street
Los Angeles, CA 90071

Kin Khao
171 Spring Street
New York, NY 10012

Local No-Chol
30869 Thousand Oaks Boulevard
Westlake Village, CA 91362

Lounge 21
Dai-ichi Hotel
1-2-6 Shimbashi
Minato-ku, Tokyo 105, Japan

Matador Bookstore Expansion
California State University
18111 Nordhoff Street
Northridge, CA 91330

McDonald's at the Denton House
2045 Jericho Turnpike
New Hyde Park, NY 11040

Metro Diner II
3001 East 11th Street
Tulsa, OK 74104

New World Coffee Shop
New World Hotel
22 Salisbury Road
Tsimshatsui Kowloon, Hong Kong

North Street Grill
661 Northern Boulevard
Great Neck, NY 11021

The Oasis Lounge Bar
The Royal Abjar Hotel
PO Box 8668
Dubai, United Arab Emirates

Panorama Restaurant
New World Hotel
22 Salisbury Road
Tsimshatsui Kowloon, Hong Kong

Papa Razzi
CambridgeSide Galleria
100 Cambridgeside Place
Cambridge, MA 02141

Pomodoro/Mirabella
17th and Parkway
Philadelphia, PA

Rasthaus Brohltal West
Germany, Highway 61
W-5476 Niederzissen

Rasthaus Leipheim
Germany, Highway 8
W-8874 Leipheim

Rasthaus Siegerland Ost
Germany, Highway 45
W-5905 Freudenberg

Rayz
CambridgeSide Galleria
100 Cambridgeside Place
Cambridge, MA 02141

Restaurant CIII
103 Waverly Place
New York, NY 10003

Rockenwagner
2435 Main Street
Santa Monica, CA 90405

The Salad Bowl
1514 Broadway
New York, NY 10036

Sfuzzi
343 Fourth Avenue
San Diego, CA 92101

Sfuzzi
4720 North Scottsdale Road
Scottsdale, AZ 85251

Sfuzzi
Union Station
50 Massachusetts Avenue, NE
Washington, DC 20001

Silver Diner
Towson Town Center
825 Dulaney Valley Road
Towson, MD 21204

Stars
Im Messeturm
Freidrich-Ebert-Anlage 49
60308 Frankfurt Am Main, Germany

Tai Pan
CambridgeSide Galleria
100 Cambridgeside Place
Cambridge, MA 02141

Trax Cafe Bar
Dai-ichi Hotel
1-2-6 Shimbashi
Minato-ku, Tokyo 105, Japan

Tropica
200 Park Avenue
New York, NY 10017

Union Bank of Switzerland
299 Park Avenue
New York, NY 10171

Union Station
39 West Jackson
Indianapolis, IN 46225

**Vaterstetten Ost und
Vaterstetten West**
Germany, Highway 99
W-8016 Feldkirchen

Vernon's Jerk Paradise
254 West 29th Street
New York, NY 10001

Vong
885 Third Avenue
New York, NY 10022

York Galleria
Box 1
York, PA 17402

Albrecht & Partner
Menterschwaigstr. 4
8000 München 90, Germany
Tel: (01149) 89-65105150
Fax: (01149) 89-640491

Arris Design
14 Imperial Place
Providence, RI 02903
Tel: (401) 274-4438
Fax: (401) 244-7517

Atelier 6 Interior
Jl. Cikini IV, 20A
Jakarta 10330, Indonesia
Tel: 0062-21-310 0276
Fax: 0062-21-310 03396

Bergmeyer Associates, Inc.
286 Congress Street
Boston, MA 02210
Tel: (617) 542-1025
Fax: (617) 338-6897

Boyd Associates
271 Grove Street
Montclair, NJ 07042
Tel: (201) 783-2878
Fax: (201) 783-1418

Brennan Beer Gorman
Monk/Interiors
515 Madison Avenue
New York, NY 10022
Tel: (212) 888-7663
Fax: (212) 935-3868

BSHA Design Group, Inc.
919 Fourth Avenue, Suite 200
San Diego, CA 92101
Tel: (619) 239-2353
Fax: (619) 239-6227

Charles Morris Mount, Inc.
300 West 108th Street
New York, NY 10025
Tel: (212) 864-2937
Fax: (212) 864-0558

Clodagh Design International
365 First Avenue
New York, NY 10010
Tel: (212) 673-9202
Fax: (212) 614-9125

Coleman/Caskey Architects, Inc.
11 Pacifica, Suite 300
Irvine, CA 92718
Tel: (714) 727-4400
Fax: (714) 727-4401

David Kellen Architect
2936 Nebraska Avenue
Santa Monica, CA 90404
Tel: (310) 452-4148
Fax: (310) 452-8351

David Turner Architects
363 Seventh Avenue, Suite 1501
New York, NY 10001
Tel: (212) 594-0840

DeRaffle Manufacturing, Inc.
2525 Palmer Avenue
New Rochelle, NY 10801
Tel: (914) 636-6850
Fax: (914) 636-6596

Design Continuum Inc.
648 Beacon Street
Boston, MA 02215
Tel: (617) 267-5115
Fax: (617) 267-3923

DiLeonardo International, Inc.
2350 Post Road
Warwick, RI 02886
Tel: (401) 732-2900
Fax: (401) 732-5315

dirk obliers design
Friedrich-Ebert-Str. 27
D-8672 Selb,Germany
Tel: (09287) 70071
Fax: (09287) 2051

Environmental Design Group, Ltd.
4090 Westown Parkway, Suite E
West Des Moines, IA 50266
Tel: (515) 224-4022
Fax: (515) 224-9254

The Fraser Nag Partnership
PO Box 1775
Dubai, United Arab Emirates
Tel: (971) 4-22-0222
Fax: (971) 4-22-6105

Frederick Brush Design
Associates Inc.
53 East Avenue
Norwalk, CT 06851
Tel: (203) 846-0828
Fax: (203) 846-2570

Gensler and Associates/Architects
1 Rockefeller Plaza, Suite 500
New York, NY 10020
Tel: (212) 581-9600
Fax: (212) 581-4593

Hatch Design Group
3198D Airport Loop Drive
Costa Mesa, CA 92626
Tel: (714) 979-8385
Fax: (714) 979-6430

Haverson/Rockwell Architects, P.C.
18 West 27th Street
New York, NY 10001
Tel: (212) 889-4182
Fax: (212) 725-2473

John E. Wheeler Architects
6455 Stichter Street
Dallas, TX 75230
Tel: (214) 987-0160
Fax: (214) 987-0409

Jordan Mozer & Associates, Ltd.
228 West Illinois Street
Chicago, IL 60610
Tel: (312) 661-0060
Fax: (312) 661-0981

K.N.W. Architects & Engineers, Ltd.
6/F North, Somerset House
28 Tong Chong Street
Quarry Bay, Hong Kong
Tel: 88801268
Fax: 8110780

Lawrence Man Architect
47-13 Cogswell Avenue
Cambridge, MA 02140
Tel: (617) 547-0374
Fax: (617) 876-8718

L. Bogdanow & Associates,
Architects
75 Spring Street
New York, NY 10012
Tel: (212) 966-0313
Fax: (212) 941-8875

Lori Freesmeier & Associates Inc.
245 East 21st Street
New York, NY 10110
Tel: (212) 533-4206
Fax: (212) 533-4206

Media Five Limited
345 Queen Street, Ninth Floor
Honolulu, HI 96813
Tel: (808) 524-2040
Fax: (808) 538-1529

Mitsubishi Estate Co., Ltd.
Third Architectural &
Engineering Dept.
4-1 Marunouchi 2-Chome
Chiyoda-ku, Tokyo 100, Japan
Tel: (03) 3287-5730
Fax: (03) 3214-7036

Morris Nathanson Design
163 Exchange Street
Pawtucket, RI 02860
Tel: (401) 723-3800
Fax: (401) 723-3813

Muzingo Associates
2288 Westwood Boulevard, Suite 210
Los Angeles, CA 90064
Tel: (310) 470-9181
Fax: (310) 470-9181

Olsen-Coffey Architects
324 East Third Street
Tulsa, OK 74120
Tel: (918) 585-1157
Fax: (918) 585-1157

Paul Draper and Associates, Inc.
4106 Swiss Avenue
Dallas, TX 75204
Tel: (214) 824-8352
Fax: (214) 824-0932

Pentagram
212 Fifth Avenue
New York, NY 10010
Tel: (212) 683-7071
Fax: (212) 532-0181

Raymond F. Fellman Architects
570 Broadway
Amityville, NY 11701
Tel: (516) 789-3555
Fax: (516) 789-3218

Sayles Graphic Design
308 Eighth Street
Des Moines, IA 50309
Tel: (515) 243-2922

SRK Architects
1225 Spring Street
Philadelphia, PA 19107
Tel: (215) 568-1090
Fax: (215) 568-1091

Steven Langford Architects
16152 Beach Boulevard, Suite 201
Huntington Beach, CA 92647
Tel: (714) 847-1189
Fax: (714) 847-4615

Studio II Architects
7758 Wisconsin Avenue, Suite 501
Bethesda, MA 22814
Tel: (301) 907-7912
Fax: (301) 907-6496

Synar•Oellien Design
Associates, Inc.
907 South Detroit Avenue
Suite 1015
Tulsa, OK 74120
Tel: (918) 749-8459
Fax: (918) 586-6284

TL Horton Design, Inc.
11120 Grader Street
Dallas, TX 75238
Tel: (214) 349-3515
Fax: (214) 348-2449

Toni Chi & Associates
215 Park Avenue South, Suite 702
New York, NY 10003
Tel: (212) 353-8860
Fax: (212) 673-1454

Valerio Simini, Architect
701 Pennsylvania Avenue, NW PH 14
Washington, DC 20004
Tel: (202) 347-0710
Fax: (202) 783-4580

PHOTOGRAPHERS

A.F. Payne Photographic
830 North Fourth Avenue
Phoenix, AZ 85003
Tel: (602) 258-3506

Joe Aker
Aker Photography
4710 Lillian Street
Houston, TX 77007
Tel: (713) 862-6343

Anthony T. Alberello
395D Blackwells Mills Road
Somerset, NJ 08873
Tel: (908) 873-0319
Fax: (908) 873-6977

Arthur Kan Photography
7 Cross Lane 1/F
Wanchai, Hong Kong
Tel: 834-1908
Fax: 838-4913

Daniel Aubry
365 First Avenue
New York, NY 10010
Tel: (212) 598-4191
Fax: (212) 505-7670

Barth Tilloston
Barth Tilloston Photography
PO Box 7697
Dallas, TX 75209
Tel: (214) 352-9590

Bill Nellans Photography
Deer Valley Studios
3800 Watermarks Parkway
Des Moines, IA 50312
Tel: (515) 274-0406
Fax: (515) 247-3371

Doug Brown
PO Box 2205
Alexandria, VA 22301
Tel: (703) 684-8778
Fax: (703) 820-5589

Lucy Chen
Lucy Chen Photography
47-13 Cogswell Avenue
Cambridge, MA 02140
Tel: (617) 547-0374
Fax: (617) 876-8718

Glenn Cormier
828 K Street, Suite 305
San Diego, CA 92101
Tel: (619) 237-5006

Deidra Davidson
2105 Havenmeyer
Redondo Beach, CA 90278
Tel: (310) 318-6554

Larry Falke
1900 MacArthur
Irvine, CA 92715
Tel: (714) 251-9407
Fax: (714) 476-4505

Wolfgang Hoyt
18 West 27th Street
New York, NY 10001
Tel: (212) 686-2569

Dennis Kan
12500 Piedmont Road
Clarksburg, MD 20871
Tel: (301) 428-9417

John Paul Kay
Jl. Gondangdia Lama Dalam 10
Jakarta 10330, Indonesia
Tel: 0062-21-310 5045
Fax: 0062-21-310 5045

Klein & Wilson Photography
2220 South Hardwood, #202
Dallas, TX 75215
Tel: (214) 421-1555

Bernhard Leniger-Salley
Albrecht & Partner
Menterschwaigstr. 4
8000 München 90, Germany
Tel: (01149) 89-65105150
Fax: (01149) 89-640491

Luminae Souter Lighting Design
1740 Army Street
San Francisco, CA 94124
Tel: (415) 285-2622
Fax: (415) 285-7718

Mary McAleer
Milroy/McAleer
711 West 11th Street, #67
Costa Mesa, CA 92627
Tel: (714) 722-6402
Fax: (714) 722-6371

Nick Merrick
Hedrich-Blessing
11 West Illinois Street
Chicago, IL 60601
Tel: (312) 321-1151
Fax: (312) 321-1165

Robert Miller
9 Hillcrest Avenue
Darien, CT 06820
Tel: (212) 246-6114

Helmut Mitter
Weintraubengasse 14/10
A-1020 Vienna, Austria
Tel: 1 21 40453

Ross Muir
75 Spring Street
New York, NY 10012
Tel: (212) 966-0313
Fax: (212) 941-8875

Dirk Obliers
Friedrich-Ebert-Str. 27
D-8672 Selb, Germany
Tel: 0049-9287-70071
Fax: 0049-9287-2051

Paul Warchol Photography
133 Mulberry Street, #65
New York, NY 10013
Tel: (212) 431-3461
Fax: (212) 274-1953

Peter Paige Associates, Inc.
269 Parkside Road
Harrington Park, NJ 07640
Tel: (201) 767-3150
Fax: (201) 767-3220

Wolfgang Pulfer
Pippingerstr. 26
8000 Münichen 60, Germany
Tel: (089) 820-5065
Fax: (089) 820-5148

Bill Robinson
PO Box 6624
San Diego, CA 92166
Tel: (619) 224-9426
Fax: (619) 224-9426

Dub Rogers
PO Box 1084
New York, NY 10028
Tel: (212) 772-2232

Ron Manville Photography
Blackstone Studios
163 Exchange Street
Pawtucket, RI 02860
Tel: (401) 723-3313
Fax: (401) 727-3220

Scott Rothstein
17 Hillvale Road
Syosset, NY 11791
Tel: (516) 531-1236

Walter Smalling
1541 Eighth Street NW
Washington, DC 20001
Tel: (202) 234-2438

Reyndell Stockman
607 South Colonial Avenue
Sterling, VA 22170
Tel: (703) 709-5824
Fax: (703) 709-5830

Tim Street-Porter
2074 Watsonia Terrace
Los Angeles, CA 90068
Tel: (213) 874-4278

Bob Swanson
Swanson Images
259 Clara Street
San Francisco, CA 94107
Tel: (415) 495-6507

Alex Vertikoff
1009 Vernon Avenue
Venice, CA 90291
Tel: (310) 450-9442
Fax: (310) 450-8882

G.u.E. von Voithenberg
Denninjerstr. 110
8000 München 81, Germany
Tel: (089) 820-5065
Fax: (089) 820-5148

Matt Wargo
4236 Main Street
Philadelphia, PA 19127
Tel: (215) 483-1211

Warren Jagger Photography, Inc.
150 Chestnut Street
Pawtucket, RI 02860
Tel: (401) 351-7366
Fax: (401) 421-7567

Reven T.C. Wurman
559 Broome Street
New York, NY 10013
Tel: (212) 925-8162
Fax: (212) 925-8162

INDEX

ACKNOWLEDGMENTS

*Without the wonderful projects illustrated on these pages there would
be no book, so thanks to all the design professionals, their clients
and photographers for sharing their talent and success.*

*My sincere appreciation and heartfelt thanks to the very able
art and editorial staff at PBC International and to
Mark Serchuck and Penny Sibal for publishing this tome.*

*A special thank you to Danny Meyer for giving his insight
to the unique world of restaurant hospitality.*